# THE
# DISSERTATION-
# TO-BOOK
# WORKBOOK

Chicago Guides
to *Writing*, **Editing**
and Publishing

*A complete list of series titles is available on the University of Chicago Press website.*

# THE DISSERTATION-TO-BOOK WORKBOOK

## EXERCISES FOR DEVELOPING AND REVISING YOUR BOOK MANUSCRIPT

Katelyn E. Knox and Allison Van Deventer

The University of Chicago Press

*Chicago and London*

The University of Chicago Press, Chicago 60637
The University of Chicago Press, Ltd., London
© 2023 by Katelyn E. Knox and Allison Van Deventer

Published 2023
Printed in the United States of America

32 31 30 29 28 27 26 25 24 23     1 2 3 4 5

ISBN-13: 978-0-226-82884-8 (cloth)
ISBN-13: 978-0-226-82581-6 (paper)
ISBN-13: 978-0-226-82885-5 (e-book)
DOI: https://doi.org/10.7208/chicago/9780226828855.001.0001

Library of Congress Cataloging-in-Publication Data

Names: Knox, Katelyn E., author. | Van Deventer, Allison, author.
Title: The dissertation-to-book workbook : exercises for developing and revising your book manuscript / Katelyn E. Knox and Allison Van Deventer.
Other titles: Chicago guides to writing, editing, and publishing.
Description: Chicago : The University of Chicago Press, 2023. | Series: Chicago guides to writing, editing, and publishing | Includes bibliographical references and index.
Identifiers: LCCN 2023001726 | ISBN 9780226828848 (cloth) | ISBN 9780226825816 (paperback) | ISBN 9780226828855 (ebook)
Subjects: LCSH: Manuscript preparation (Authorship) | Manuscripts—Editing. | Dissertations, Academic.
Classification: LCC PN160 .K56 2023 | DDC 808.02—dc23/eng/20230412
LC record available at https://lccn.loc.gov/2023001726

♾ This paper meets the requirements of ANSI/NISO Z39.48-1992 (Permanence of Paper).

# CONTENTS

# The What, Why, and How of This Workbook

You're writing your first academic book. You've read all the advice books; you've written a dissertation; you may even have attended webinars on how to write your proposal and pitch your book to publishers. You know you need to revise what you have. But when you sit down at your desk, what do you actually *do*?

This workbook is the answer. In a series of practical, actionable steps, we show you how to distill your core argument, discover an organizational schema that works, and recognize what each chapter adds to the story. We even give you a method for drafting and revising new material. By the end, you'll have a solid understanding of what you need to prioritize, how to thread your core ideas through each chapter, and what work remains to be done. If you're looking for a way to grasp your book's big picture and use what you learn to guide your revision process, this workbook is for you.

At the heart of this workbook is the process of writing what we call "book questions" and "chapter answers": two or three core questions that receive a one-sentence answer for each chapter. This framework, as you'll see, is a powerful tool for aligning your book's evidence with its claims. As you work with your book questions and chapter answers, you'll discover how to evaluate your book's narrative arc, express its significance, articulate its organizing principle, and assess your chapters' variability along multiple dimensions. You'll poke at your terminology and play with your chapter order. In the end, this framework will lead to a sharpened book argument, a compelling narrative arc, chapters that tangibly advance your book's claims, and, most importantly, confidence about all aspects of your project.

This workbook is designed for scholars in the humanities and qualitative social sciences who have monograph manuscripts already in progress. We wrote it with dissertation-to-book authors in mind because authors at this stage face the uniquely challenging task of rethinking a huge amount of draft material without the experience of having written a book before. But it can be useful to anyone who has a critical mass of draft writing: notes, conference and seminar papers, journal articles, rough writing, dissertation chapters, and so on. We've found that the exercises are most effective if you have draft material corresponding to about 50 percent of your future book, excluding your introduction and conclusion. That is, these exercises work best when you already have some writing, not when you merely have an *idea* for a book. We also assume you are writing for publication with an English-language academic publisher (a university press or academic trade press).

If you meet these criteria, we expect you'll find value in this workbook, whether you're revising your dissertation, writing a first book that isn't based on a dissertation, writing a second or third book, or returning to your dissertation later in your career. If you wrote your dissertation as a book manuscript from the beginning and so don't expect it to need major changes, this workbook will help you clarify and confirm your choices so that you're ready to pitch them to publishers.

## THIS WORKBOOK'S ORIGINS

We're Katelyn and Allison, and we have years of experience helping scholars navigate the messy process of writing books. We met in graduate school and became friends and writing partners. Katelyn is an associate professor of French at the University of Central Arkansas, and Allison is a developmental editor who works with academic clients. Based on her experience of writing and publishing her first book with Liverpool University Press, Katelyn created an online curriculum for first-time book authors—what she wished had existed when she was going through the process—and brought Allison on board to help run it as a summer workshop conducted over Zoom.

In the workshop's subsequent iterations, we tested the core exercises with hundreds of projects, brought to us by authors from all kinds of situations and with a wide variety of challenges. Based on what we learned, we repeatedly revised the curriculum. The result is this workbook. Our careful development process means that this curriculum works for most humanities and qualitative social sciences book projects, regardless of the field, discipline, or author profile. Because we've taken so many authors through this curriculum, we're confident that it's systematic enough to help you produce a strong, cohesive book project, regardless of what shape your manuscript is in or how well equipped you feel to tackle it. Alums of our workshops have called this process "hugely clarifying." They often find they can produce a book proposal with ease and can immediately see what to cut and what to keep in their chapters.

## AN OVERVIEW OF THE WORK YOU'LL DO

The work you'll undertake is divided into two parts. In the first, which we call "working *on*" your book, you'll engage in critical pre-revision thinking about numerous dimensions of your book project. You'll describe, evaluate, and make plans for your book, but you won't revise any of your manuscript's actual prose. Above all, the exercises in chapters 1–13 are designed to help you develop a clear book argument via an unconventional route, centered on your "book questions" and "chapter answers." As you'll see over the course of this work, academic books can feel unwieldy and complex, and arguments have a lot of points to hit. Your book's argument needs to articulate your book's main idea, but not at the expense of being cut off from its evidence and organization. Conversely, your book's main ideas define what evidence your book will use and how it will be structured. This workbook helps you take a balanced approach to producing your book's argument by telescoping between the book's various scales and toggling between the different major points of the argument. In the end—in chapter 12, to be precise—you'll discover that a book argument is rarely something you can capture simply by sitting down to complete the sentence "In this book, I argue . . ." Instead, your argument is shaped over time as you consider all the dimensions of your book and its chapters. When you work this way, you'll find that your argument is not so much "articulated" as it is "assembled"—a discovery that often brings huge relief.

After chapter 13, you'll transition to what we call "working *in*" your book—revising your draft. In chapters 14–16, you'll revise your chapters to serve your book and learn how to work quickly and efficiently to produce any remaining chapters.

## HOW THIS WORKBOOK INVITES YOU TO WORK

Unlike other advice about turning dissertations into books, this workbook marries description with targeted, narrow prompts and reflection exercises that will move you beyond *thinking* into *doing*. Authors have found this aspect of the workbook enormously reassuring—all you have to do is sit down and work on the exercises in order, step by step.[1] What's more, we give you specific examples of book projects (all invented or anonymized) to help you understand what you're aiming for. Finally, we give you rough estimates of how long the exercises should take, a few sorting checkpoints to help you skip over exercises that are not relevant for your project, and practical ways to assess whether the revisions you're envisioning are realistic given your time constraints and professional aspirations. Above all, this work is designed to fit into your life—whatever your career stage or professional responsibilities.

But we're certainly not going to say this work is easy or comfortable. Our live workshops have taught us that authors can succeed in completing these exercises if they persist despite the discomfort and uncertainty that inevitably arise. In our experience, four key practices set authors up for the highest chances of success. Throughout this workbook, we'll encourage you to engage in these practices.

### Practice 1: Prioritize Action

Merely reading and thinking about this workbook's exercises will not produce a more coherent book. You must complete the activities, however provisionally.

### Practice 2: Aim for Progress, Not Perfection

Over and over in this workbook, we invite you to make your work just good enough for now and then move on. Most alums of the live workshops point to this practice as the cornerstone of their ability to produce a strong book. Specifically, they say that the exercises ask challenging questions and at times raise doubts about aspects of the project. As a result, you might feel called to spend dozens of hours trying to definitively resolve these uncertainties in an attempt to perfect your work.

But just as thinking without action will not result in a finished book draft, neither will spending more than the recommended amount of time on each project conception task (chapters 1–13). During this work, you might feel that we ask you to move on too quickly. Those time limits are there by design: we *want* you to produce imperfect work and then come back to revise it in later chapters. When you revisit your work from new angles, you'll gain insight that would have eluded you if you had attempted to perfect your work at an earlier stage.

### Practice 3: Reflect Intentionally and Capture Doubts

At the end of each chapter, we give you space to record your thoughts and nagging doubts about your book project. This practice serves two functions. First, it supports the previous one: to persist despite uncertainty, you need to deliberately capture those doubts and return to them later. Second, reflecting on your evolving book at regular intervals generates a record of how your thinking matures over time. While some authors' projects change radically because of this work, others' books change in much subtler—but no less significant—compounding ways. As you'll likely find, sharpened thinking often emerges not through macro-scale actions like cutting a chapter, but through small tweaks.

### Practice 4: Build Confidence by Asking Challenging Questions

One of our workshop alums put it best: comparing her book project to a house of cards, she admitted that she hesitated to interrogate certain dimensions for fear that doing so would topple the entire project. She believed that as long as she didn't probe her project too much—push too hard on any of the individual cards—the somewhat shaky foundation could remain standing. With support and reassurance, she courageously turned toward these dimensions of her project and discovered that even if some cards fell, asking the hard questions ultimately made her project stronger. Her book is now forthcoming with her dream publisher.

Many of this workbook's exercises ask pointed, challenging questions about your book—questions many authors would prefer to avoid. Keep in mind, however, that these are often the same questions peer reviewers will ask about your manuscript. Though they're uncomfortable, asking these questions will result in a better-thought-out project and, above all, more confidence in what you produce.

## WHAT YOU WON'T DO IN THIS WORKBOOK

No book can do everything, and this workbook is no exception. Here's what this book *won't* help you do.

### Decide Whether to Publish a Book or Articles

This workbook assumes that you've already made the decision—whatever the reason—to pursue monograph publication. If you aren't yet certain about this decision, please consult chapters 2, 3, and 4 of William Germano's *From Dissertation to Book*, which cover this issue in great detail.[2]

### Answer Questions about Your Book's Publishability or Your Argument's Significance

A general curriculum such as this one can't address the publishing norms of every discipline or field. Once you've completed the exercises, you will have produced material suitable to send to scholars and mentors in your field, who will be able to assess your study's publishability, your claims' significance, and your book's rigor.

### Complete Your Book Manuscript

After completing chapters 14–15, you will have rough drafts of the body sections of your body chapters. We do not, however, address the introduction or conclusion to your body chapters, nor do we address writing the introduction or conclusion to your book itself.

### Copyedit Your Book's Prose

In this workbook, we won't teach you to line-edit your draft or improve your writing style. For one reason, others teach these skills better than we can. For another, polishing a book manuscript's language is less important in the pre-peer-review stage than most authors think it is. Your writing needs to be precise enough to convey what you really mean and standard enough that a variety of readers can understand it easily. To get past peer review, it does not have to be flawless (whatever that means). It's much more important to invest in sharpening your book's argument and clarifying its structure. And yes, if English isn't your first language—we mean you too! Most of you are just as capable of getting your point across in English as native speakers are.

This book focuses on big-picture tasks: figuring out your book's structure, clarifying your arguments, and evaluating chapters to see whether and how they fit. The later chapters help you draft the body sections of your chapters and foreground your voice. Above all, you can think of this workbook as a tool you can use to substantially revise your book and its core body chapters. The work you'll do is similar to what a developmental editor would do. Unlike copyeditors, developmental editors ask about the big picture: the main ideas, structure, logic, and organization. But hiring a developmental editor isn't financially feasible for everyone, and even if you do choose to work with one, you'll get more value from their work if you've done significant big-picture thinking first. In its focus on major revision, this workbook is similar to two of William Germano's books on academic writing: *On Revision: The Only Writing That Counts*, which helps you revise any piece of academic writing, and his more specific *From Dissertation to Book*, which walks you through general exercises to help you sift through your raw dissertation material.[3]

For superb advice on style and voice, see Eric Hayot's *The Elements of Academic Style: Writing for the Humanities*, Joseph M. Williams's *Style: Lessons in Clarity and Grace*, and Helen Sword's *Stylish Academic Writing*.[4]

### Identify Your Book's Target Audience and Possible Publishers

These tasks deserve more space than we can give them in this workbook. They are covered in Laura Portwood-Stacer's *The Book Proposal Book: A Guide for Scholarly Authors*, William Germano's *Getting It Published: A Guide for Scholars and Anyone Else Serious about Serious Books*, and Beth Luey's *Revising Your Dissertation: Advice from Leading Editors*.[5]

### Draft Your Book Proposal

Although you'll be able to draw from the writing you produce in this workbook when you draft your book proposal, the proposal is a distinct genre with its own norms and requirements. For an excellent guide to writing book proposals, see Laura Portwood-Stacer's *The Book Proposal Book: A Guide for Scholarly Authors*.[6]

### Gain Procedural Information on Publication

This material too has been better covered elsewhere. See William Germano's *Getting It Published: A Guide for Scholars and Anyone Else Serious about Serious Books*, Beth Luey's *Revising Your Dissertation: Advice from Leading Editors*, and Laura Portwood-Stacer's *The Book Proposal Book: A Guide for Scholarly Authors*.[7]

## HOW TO USE THIS WORKBOOK

### Completing the Workbook Exercises

Because this workbook's exercises are iterative, you should work through the material from start to finish. As we explained above, merely *reading* and *thinking* (abstractly) about the ideas in this workbook won't produce a stronger book. Instead, you should complete the activities in order. At several key moments, we include sorting checkpoints so you can ensure you're ready to proceed.

During our live workshops, we always recommended that the authors write out their responses to the activities by hand, if they could. Those who did so consistently reported that the ability to scribble, cross things out, draw arrows, and sketch out notes helped them banish perfectionism and generate more interesting insights. We encourage you to write on these pages.

This workbook assumes that you're at an early stage of revising your book manuscript. But the exercises still work even if you're slightly later or earlier in the process. Here's how to tailor this workbook if you find yourself in any of the following common situations:

**If you already have a contract**: If you've already signed a contract with a publisher, or if you're in any other situation that means you can't change your book structure much, then do the chapters in sequence, but move quickly through chapters 1, 2, 7, and 11, skipping any written activities that seem to rehash thinking you've already done. Skim chapters 13, 14, 15, and 16 and do only what seems useful.

**If you still need to research and draft two or more full chapters**: In this case, complete chapters 1 and 2. Then do chapters 3–8, but try to stay on the lower end of the suggested times—your answers may change later, so they don't need to be polished. Feel free to leave blanks in the exercises if you don't yet know the answers. After chapter 8, take a break from the workbook to do more research for your planned chapters, and then complete chapter 14 and steps 1 and 2 of chapter 15. If you want more strategies for drafting, read appendix E. When you have all of your chapters drafted, do chapters 9–13 and finally the rest of chapters 15 and 16.

**If less than 50 percent of your book has been drafted**: You might be in this situation if your book isn't based on a dissertation. By "drafted," though, we mean any writing you've already completed—it could be a dissertation, conference papers, journal articles, research notes, and so on. Be generous with yourself when assessing how much you've completed; it doesn't have to be polished or focused. If you genuinely have less than 50 percent of your book covered in some kind of draft, then simply read through chapters 1, 2, 6, and 7 and think about the concepts—you don't need to complete the exercises. To draft preliminary chapters, complete chapter 14 and steps 1 and 2 of chapter 15. If you want more strategies for drafting, read appendix E. Once you've drafted a good chunk of material, you can return to chapter 1 and work through the entire workbook as written.

**If you wrote your dissertation as a book**: If you wrote your dissertation with an eye to the book it would become, you may be happy with its current structure and argument. We think you'll still find these exercises helpful and clarifying. You might not have realized it at the time, but writing your dissertation involved making dozens of decisions that shaped your book-in-becoming's argument and story. Even if you don't make any major changes to your manuscript after completing this workbook, the exercises will help you assess whether the implicit decisions you made truly work for your book, and they'll show you how to highlight and explain your book's strengths. If you're in this situation, we recommend that you do the entire curriculum, but you can treat the exercises as more confirmatory than exploratory where it seems appropriate. Don't, however, rush through the activities that ask you to probe your terminology in chapter 9, steps 2 and 3, and chapter 10, step 1.

## Recommended Pacing

This workbook's exercises can be completed in an intense burst (by working three to four hours per day during a break from other responsibilities), but authors tend to fare best when they work more steadily over a longer period (five to ten hours per week). The targeted activities are designed to fit alongside your regular teaching and service responsibilities. Throughout the exercises, we also give authors who need to publish a book for tenure ways of ensuring that their work is possible given their externally imposed deadlines.

| Chapter | Estimated Hours | Max Hours |
|---------|-----------------|-----------|
| 1 | 3 | 5 |
| 2 | 3 | 4 |
| 3 | 2 | 3 |
| 4 | 2 | 4 |
| 5 | 3 | 5 |
| 6 | 4 | 6 |
| 7 | 4 | 6 |
| 8 | 3 | 5 |
| 9 | 5 | 8 |
| 10 | 5 | 8 |
| 11 | 3 | 5 |
| 12 | 3 | 5 |
| 13 | 6 | 10 |
| TOTAL | 46 | 74 |

Many authors who are working during the academic year find it feasible to complete the first two chapters in one week, and then one chapter every week thereafter (for a total of twelve weeks). But because each project and each author's personal and professional obligations are unique, we're limiting our recommendations to the number of total hours to spend on each chapter's exercises. You could easily spend five or ten times the number of hours on each chapter, but doing so wouldn't mean you'd produce better work. Respect the time limit for each workbook chapter and move on, even if you don't feel ready, because the curriculum is iterative. This table gives an overview of how you can expect to spend your time in chapters 1–13.

In chapters 14–16 (working *in* your book), you'll assemble and revise your book's core chapters using systematic strategies. The amount of time you'll spend revising will depend on the state of your current material and the extent and nature of your revisions.

## A FINAL NOTE: YOU AREN'T ALONE!

If there's one thing we've learned from leading dissertation-to-book workshops and mentoring hundreds of authors with book projects at very different stages, it's that many authors feel alone. You may feel that you're the only one with your particular book challenges. We promise that while your book will certainly be unique, your challenges—and your feeling of aloneness!—are widely shared.

If you're a first-time author, you may worry that your book is just a collection of chapters, with no clear overarching argument. Or you may have an argument, but you aren't certain your chapters are supporting it thoroughly—the chapters keep wandering off into fascinating tangents of their own. Maybe you have reviewer reports and even a book contract, but you don't know what to prioritize when you start to implement the feedback.

You may be early in the book-writing process and want to make sure you don't waste time, or you may have been spinning your wheels for a while, unsure how to make decisions and move forward. Or maybe you just aren't convinced that what you have adds up to a book.

Such doubts may be compounded if you, like so many authors, lack the support and mentorship that such a complex project demands. Women scholars, scholars working on interdisciplinary projects, Black scholars, Indigenous scholars, other scholars of color, disabled scholars, LGBTQ+ scholars, trans and nonbinary scholars, scholars whose first language isn't English, scholars who've immigrated to the United States, scholars at rural or underfunded institutions, scholars in alt-ac careers, adjuncts, independent scholars, parents of young and/or high-needs children, neurodivergent scholars, scholars who've had to break ties with their mentors, scholars from poor or working-class backgrounds, first-generation scholars, scholars with heavy teaching loads—if you belong to any (or several!) of these categories, you may not have the close, supportive network and abundant resources you deserve as you bring your book into the world.

But you don't have to figure it out alone. This workbook will help you understand what makes academic books work and will show you, in straightforward steps, how to clarify for your readers what your book has been saying all along. Over and over, we've seen authors in our workshops, many of whom fit several of the descriptions above, find their core arguments and ultimately publish their books. We wish we could give you access to every resource you could possibly need to complete your book. Because we can't, we've done our best to demystify the features of strong academic monographs, in the hope that all scholars—but especially those who are marginalized for any reason—will be empowered to intervene with confidence in their fields.

We also wish we could give you the same live, personalized support and encouragement we offer during these workshops. In their place, we've given you glimpses of common hurdles faced by the hundreds of authors who have used our materials, plus the same advice, recommendations, and encouragement we give them. You'll find them in the "Common Discoveries," "Common Stumbling Blocks," and "Debrief, Support, and Troubleshooting" sections at the beginning and end of each chapter. We hope these features of the workbook will support you along the way. And even if you never meet us, we're cheering for you.

## CHAPTER 1

# Considering Your Book on Its Own Terms

## WHAT TO EXPECT

In chapters 1–13, you will telescope between different levels of your book. This chapter's activities focus squarely on the book level. You'll begin to see your project both as a collection of ideas that do work within your discipline and as an intellectual object whose features (such as evidence, framing, and scope) dictate the type of work it can do.

### Time Investment

Expect to spend **3–4 hours**, cumulatively, on the exercises in this chapter. **Do not spend more than 5 hours** on them. Remember that this curriculum is iterative, so work quickly and move on, even if you aren't fully satisfied with what you produce. If necessary, pretend you have a nonnegotiable meeting with us by the end of this week (or tomorrow, if you're working on an accelerated plan) and you must submit your work to receive feedback.

### Common Discoveries in Chapter 1

- **A new understanding of what academic books are and do**. Most authors have unrealistically high expectations for what books—especially first books—must be and do. Additionally, while authors might understand that the claims they can make in articles (and other relatively short pieces) depend on the evidence they mobilize, books somehow feel different. This chapter reminds you that books are no different: the claims you can make depend on the evidence you mobilize.
- **A sense that your comparative project might need to be a single-focus project**. Because these exercises ask you to tie claims to evidence, some authors wonder whether their book will be stronger with a narrower focus.
- **Confidence that your ideas are book-worthy**. Most authors begin these exercises with only a vague sense that their ideas work as a book. This chapter helps you articulate what your book is and does, which allows you to evaluate whether your book works as a complete whole.

### Common Stumbling Blocks

Let's review a few common difficulties that authors encounter in this workbook and in this chapter in particular.

- **Writing too much**. This workbook intentionally constrains your writing to force you to prioritize your ideas, which in turn will guide you to produce a more coherent book.

- **Aiming for perfection**. These exercises are iterative. In fact, in chapter 11, you will revisit and refine the material you produce here. Aim to get your material 80 percent solid. Do not work for more than 5 cumulative hours on this chapter's exercises.

- **Treating the activities as confirmatory rather than exploratory**. Remember this workbook's fourth practice: building confidence through asking hard questions. To do so successfully, you'll need to approach your book (and these activities) with the right mindset: hold your current understanding of your book lightly, approach your book with curiosity, and demonstrate willingness to interrogate many of your book's dimensions. Those who approach these exercises in an exploratory mode tend to make choices that, while difficult, produce stronger, more coherent books.

- **Worrying that your book's scope is too narrow (or asking broader questions about your study's publishability)**. A lot of dissertation-to-book advice, including advice from editors and mentors, assumes that most dissertations are too narrow in scope to work as academic monographs. In this chapter, however, you'll learn that broadening your project's scope without asking questions about your evidence base can lead to serious problems. We'll help you avoid these problems by focusing not on how "broad" or "narrow" your book is, but on how well aligned your book's scope, claims, and evidence are. Editors, though, *will* eventually assess whether your book is too broad or narrow for their list. Because this dimension is highly field- and press-dependent—for instance, monographs about a single novel are often too narrow for most university presses to publish, but monographs on a single event could be fine for history lists—you will need to solicit feedback on the scope of your project, given the publishing norms in your field.

- **Feeling anxious about your study's significance**. In this chapter, we ask you to lay out a few key dimensions of your project, including a quick note about why your book's intellectual contributions matter. This is merely to get a quick sense of your understanding of your book *at this time*. In later chapters, you'll consider this dimension in more depth. If this prompt provokes anxiety, just write something provisional and move on.

## EXERCISES

### Step 1: Describing Your Book on Its Own Terms

In this step, you'll lay out key information about your book. Depending on where you are in your understanding of your book project, writing down this information might be difficult. If it is, don't panic! Just do what you can given your understanding of the project right now. By the end of this workbook, you should have a much better idea of what to say.

First, consider the following examples.

**LITERARY STUDIES**

| My book's topic: | Travel in nineteenth-century British literature |
|---|---|
| What my book does in its discipline: | My book defines travel broadly in nineteenth-century British literature by bringing together imagined international travel, international travelogues, and country-to-city novels. |

| What my book does not do: | My book does not pretend to be an overview of nineteenth-century British literature, and it does not offer a history of travel within and beyond the British Empire. |
|---|---|
| Why doing this intellectual work matters: | Considering travel in this broader way allows for more complex understandings of how travel operates in relation to the nation at this time. |
| The main question my book asks is: | How are different forms of travel narratives in nineteenth-century Britain mobilized in service of different narratives of nationhood? |
| To answer this question, I [methodology and evidence base]: | I apply traditional literary analysis to both travel writings and canonical novels. |
| Overall, my book's main idea, claim, or intervention is: | That defining travel in this broad way allows for a more nuanced understanding of the relationship between movement and nation in this time period. |

## INTERNATIONAL DIPLOMACY STUDIES

| My book's topic: | The role non-state actors (especially NGOs) can play in international diplomacy |
|---|---|
| What my book does in its discipline: | My book studies how a Christian NGO, [name], successfully engages in international diplomacy.* |
| What my book does not do: | My book is most interested in examining NGO actions and, as a result, does not pretend to offer an in-depth examination of these relations from the state side of things. |
| Why doing this intellectual work matters: | If we understand what makes [name] successful, it can serve as a model for other transnational NGOs to emulate, thereby improving international diplomacy. |
| The main question my book asks is: | What do successful NGOs do to facilitate international diplomacy? |
| To answer this question, I [methodology and evidence base]: | I study different dimensions of a Christian NGO, [name], comparing it organizationally to other transnational NGOs. |
| Overall, my book's main idea, claim, or intervention is: | That [name] can serve as a model for other successful transnational NGOs in [three ways]. |

*Note that this statement is less strong than the previous or following examples because it lacks information about how the book advances conversations in its discipline.

## HISTORY

| My book's topic: | Labor rights and grassroots labor initiatives in post-1989 Baltic states |
|---|---|
| What my book does in its discipline: | My book introduces individuals' conceptions of labor rights—and corporations' alignment or not with them—as a crucial (heretofore ignored) variable in understanding the region's economic history. |
| What my book does not do: | My book is a grassroots, bottom-up history. As a result, it draws on economic and labor policy documents and legislation from the time, but it prioritizes oral history sources and individual corporations' policies and publications. It does not pretend to be a comprehensive labor history of post-1989 Baltic states. |
| Why doing this intellectual work matters: | This study illustrates the profound ground-up impact that individual actors can have. |

| The main question my book asks is: | How, why, and to what extent do corporations align their policies with individuals' understandings of labor rights in the Baltic states after 1989, and what impact do these alignments have? |
| --- | --- |
| To answer this question, I [methodology and evidence base]: | I study federal labor laws, national economic markers, oral histories and interviews with individual workers and corporate officials from [three major companies], and court proceedings between workers and those three corporations. |
| Overall, my book's main idea, claim, or intervention is: | That when these corporations make a visible effort to align their policies with individual workers' understandings of labor rights, which most did following workers' grassroots initiatives in 2001, there is a marked uptick in national economic markers. |

Now it's your turn. Complete the following table:

| My book's topic: | |
| --- | --- |
| What my book does in its discipline: | |
| What my book does not do: | |
| Why doing this intellectual work matters: | |
| The main question my book asks is: | |
| To answer this question, I [methodology and evidence base]: | |
| Overall, my book's main idea, claim, or intervention is: | |

## Step 2: Understanding the Alignment between Scope, Claims, and Evidence

If you've never written a book before, it may be hard to realistically assess your book's scope. One key idea to grasp is that the claims you can make and your evidence base are interdependent: to make broad claims, you need a broad and diverse evidence base, whereas a narrow evidence base can support only limited claims. Neither broad claims nor narrow claims are inherently "good" or "bad."

Much of the advice for dissertation-to-book authors contends that the first step in revising a dissertation into a publishable book is to widen its scope.[1] While you'll eventually need to confer with mentors regarding your book's scope and its chances of publication (and below we'll give some general tips about scopes that might be too narrow), you shouldn't automatically assume that broadening the book's scope is the best thing to do. Reviewers and editors will likely criticize a book if its evidence base is not proportional to the claims it makes. In other words, what's most important is whether your claims and scope are *aligned*. Above all, your central idea needs to be anchored in and supported by the evidence you actually have (or will have).

In this step, we'll guide you to think like an editor or peer reviewer who's focusing on your book's claims, scope, and evidence base. To quickly assess your book, this reader will ask: *Are the claims the author makes appropriate given the book's scope and evidence?*

Let's review a few examples and predict what an editor's or reviewer's reactions might be. For this exercise, we're going to consider only the topic, question, and evidence base.

### INTERNATIONAL DIPLOMACY STUDIES

| | |
|---|---|
| My book's topic: | The role non-state actors (especially NGOs) can play in international diplomacy |
| My book's main question: | What do successful NGOs do to facilitate international diplomacy? |
| My book's main examples or case studies: | One Christian transnational NGO is the central case study; each chapter analyzes a different dimension of it and compares it to other transnational NGOs. |

The author asserts that her book's main purpose is to make broad claims about non-state actors' roles in international diplomacy. But she uses one Christian NGO as her main example. How do you think an editor will answer the question "Are the claims the author makes appropriate given the book's scope and evidence base?"

Even if the author does compare the Christian NGO to others in each chapter, the editor will notice that she bases her claims on a single case study of one Christian NGO. The editor will certainly wonder: Are any conclusions one might draw from studying this one religiously affiliated NGO actually generalizable to many other non-state actors? The book's claims, that is, are likely broader than the evidence base can support.

Books that make relatively narrow claims can still run into trouble if their claims are misaligned with their evidence. For instance, the claim may not be thoroughly supported by the *type* of evidence that's being offered. Consider these examples:

### LITERARY STUDIES

| | |
|---|---|
| My book's topic: | The way troubadour poetry impacted sociopolitical debates |

| My book's main question: | How did troubadour poetry impact sociopolitical debates? |
|---|---|
| My book's main examples or case studies: | Canonical works by five troubadours |

Now reflect on this book from your editorial perspective—are the claims the author can make appropriate given the book's scope and evidence base?

Notice that this author's evidence doesn't seem appropriate for the types of claims she's making. She would definitely be able to make claims in the opposite direction—that is, about how sociopolitical debates play out in troubadour poetry or how troubadour poetry represents sociopolitical debates—but without much more robust historical evidence, she is unlikely to be able to support claims about how troubadour poetry impacted sociopolitical debates.

Here are some examples of a different problem commonly found in projects that focus on real people or groups.

### HISTORY

| My book's topic: | The second wave of emigration from the Eastern Bloc, 1986–1987 |
|---|---|
| My book's main question: | How did individuals and organizations materially impact the varied experiences of refugees? |
| My book's main examples or case studies: | Archives of operational and policy documents from five different international organizations and governments |

Notice the subtle disconnect between the main question and the book's case studies. Whereas the question implies that the book will focus on refugees' lived experiences, the evidence suggests that the story the book is most able to tell is about the organizations' and governments' initiatives, *not* the refugees *per se*.

The author should ask whether they actually have the evidence to answer this refugee-focused question, or whether they should revise their question to better fit the evidence they have.

### SOCIOLOGY

| My book's topic: | Community gardens in four US communities in the 1990s |
|---|---|
| My book's main question: | How do community gardens generate what I call *actifoodism*, a suite of economic, social, and environmental justice activities? |
| My book's main examples or case studies: | Participant interviews with community gardeners, city officials, and food supply chain workers |

This book's main question and examples seem better aligned. But the author should reflect on their book's main actor. Do the participant interviews allow them to center the "community gardens" themselves, or are "community gardeners" (the people) the main focus of the book?

The history and sociology examples are two sides of the same problem. In the history example, the author seems to want to focus on the *people*, but has evidence for the larger *systems.* In the sociology example, the author seems to want to focus on the broader *thing*, but likely has evidence for the *people*. Both authors could decide to do additional research to find the evidence they would need to answer their book's main question. But doing so would require time and resources. Before making a decision, they should consider whether they could revise their question to match their evidence.

Now it's time to assess what an editor will "hear" if you present her with the answers you produced earlier. Flip back to review your answers. Then answer the questions below.

| My book's topic: | |
|---|---|
| My book's main question: | |
| My book's main examples or case studies: | |
| Are the claims I make appropriate given the book's scope and evidence base? | |

---

*Want Additional Practice?* - - - - - - - - - - - - - - - - - - - - - - - - - - - - - - - - - - - - - - - - - - - - - -

Any time you undertake a new mode of writing, it's useful to have a successful model to deconstruct. We strongly recommend that you identify at least one model book. Throughout this workbook, we'll suggest targeted ways to analyze it.

To select an appropriate model book, first choose a press for which you think your project would be a good fit. Then review the books it has published in your field in the past five to ten years. Find a few monographs (not edited volumes) similar to yours in scope and methodology (not necessarily topic). Then research the author of each book to identify which books are *first* books. Choose at least one first book to serve as your model throughout this workbook. (If you're writing your second or third book, you may want to look for models written at career stages similar to yours.)

Once you've found a model book, assess the fit between its claims, scope, and evidence base.

> **SORTING CHECKPOINT**
>
> If you decide that your claims, scope, and evidence base are reasonably well aligned (or could quickly be made so by simply revising your book's main question), revise your question and proceed to step 4. For additional exercises to assess the terms you use to describe your scope, see appendix B. If you think you need to do *major* work to align them better, or if revising your question in this way would produce a book based on a single case study, work, or author, proceed to step 3.

## Step 3: Troubleshooting Misaligned Claims, Scope, and Evidence

When you have a serious mismatch between your book's claims and evidence that can't be fixed merely by quickly revising your main question or the terms you use to describe your book's scope (using the exercises in appendix B), you can choose one of two general solutions: narrow your book's question to match your evidence or broaden your evidence to match your question.

Here's how the author of the NGO book would implement each solution.

### OPTION 1: REVISING TOPIC AND SCOPE TO MATCH EVIDENCE

The author could narrow her topic and question to match the evidence she actually has and revise her work.

| My book's topic: | ~~The role non-state actors (especially NGOs) can play in international diplomacy~~ The effective practices of one Christian transnational NGO in participating in international diplomacy |
|---|---|
| My book's main question: | ~~What do successful NGOs do to facilitate international diplomacy?~~ What characteristics and practices allow Christian NGO [name] to successfully participate in international diplomacy in [context], and to what extent might these characteristics and practices serve different types of NGOs (religiously affiliated or not, smaller or larger than [name]) in different geographical contexts? |
| My book's main examples or case studies: | One Christian transnational NGO is the central case study; each chapter analyzes a different dimension of it and compares it to other transnational NGOs. |

Now reflect on this new book from the editorial perspective—are the claims the author makes appropriate given the book's scope and evidence base? What other questions or reservations do you, in your fictional role as editor, now have about this project?

In our view, this book's claims are much better aligned with its evidence base. However, an editor or reviewer might ask why answering this narrower question requires an entire monograph. Since the scope is now so narrow, the author should consider checking with a trusted mentor regarding the project's publishability as a monograph, especially if she is on the tenure track.

### OPTION 2: REVISING EVIDENCE TO MATCH TOPIC AND SCOPE

She could continue to pursue the more general topic and broader question, which will entail broadening her evidence base.

| My book's topic: | The role non-state actors (especially NGOs) can play in international diplomacy |
|---|---|

| My book's main question: | What do successful NGOs do to facilitate international diplomacy? |
|---|---|
| My book's main examples or case studies: | The Christian transnational NGO will become one case study among many. Each chapter will center on a characteristic of NGOs that successfully engage in international diplomacy and illustrate how this characteristic manifests in a diverse range of NGOs (religiously affiliated and not; small and large, etc.). |

Now reflect on this new book from the editorial perspective—are the claims the author makes appropriate given the book's scope and evidence base?

Review the changes the author envisions. Imagine that a good friend told you they were going to undertake this project. How would you respond? What other questions or reservations do you have about this project?

Notice that pursuing this project will involve fundamentally restructuring her book and will likely require extensive additional research. To find the additional case studies and develop new analyses will take years—time the author might not have.

When it comes to your book, there is no universal "right" fix for misaligned claims, scope, and evidence. However, because finding and analyzing new evidence and drafting chapters from scratch is extremely time-consuming, it's wise for authors who need the book for their tenure dossier to assume they need to select option 1: narrowing their topic, question, and scope to fit their evidence.

The only case in which doing so is not necessarily a good idea is when the resulting book would consist of a single case study (author, text, etc.) or would become so narrow that it would no longer warrant an entire monograph.

| I plan to . . . | ☐ Revise the claims to match the evidence I have | ☐ Broaden the evidence or shift the evidence base to match the claims | ☐ A combination of broadening/shifting evidence and revising claims |
|---|---|---|---|
| Common concerns: | ☐ The resulting project will consist of only one case study. | | ☐ Broadening or shifting the evidence will take years. |
| What other questions or reservations do you have about this revised project? | | | |

Finally, produce an updated table that reflects your most current thinking:

| My book's topic: | |
|---|---|
| My book's main question: | |
| My book's main examples or case studies: | |

## Step 4: Freewriting to Assess Your Book as a Book

Before you invest hundreds of hours in this project, you'll want to make sure that your book works (or at least could work) *as a book* in two main ways: *scope* and *coherence*.

### SCOPE

Think back to the Christian NGO example. If the author continues with her book's narrow scope, focusing on only one Christian NGO, wouldn't an article-length piece—or, at the most, two articles—be sufficient to make those claims? Why does the work that the book does for and in its field(s) require the space of a book?

### COHERENCE

Now let's think about the study of travel narratives in nineteenth-century British literature. Do all of its chapters build up to a compelling, book-length argument? Or are they essentially independent case studies that happen to coalesce around a central theme? In other words, what larger story emerges from a book about these narratives that could not be replicated in a series of independent articles?

Freewrite (write to explore what you really think, without worrying about your prose being read by anyone) on the following prompts:

| | |
|---|---|
| Scope (1 paragraph): Why does the work of this book require a book format? (Be especially thorough in your justification if your book consists primarily of a single case study, author, etc.) | |
| Coherence (1 paragraph): What larger point can you make by studying these cases together in a single book that you could not make by considering them in independent articles? | |

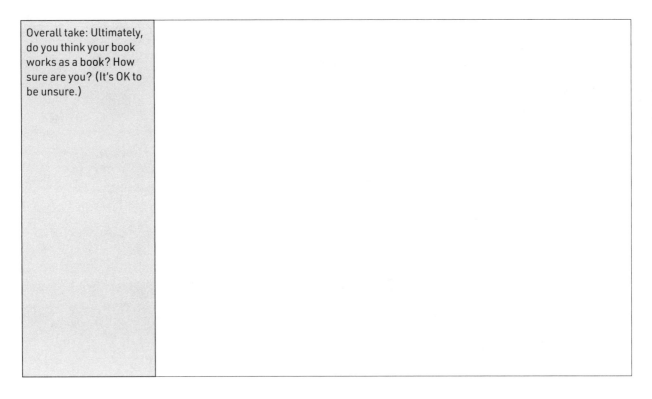

Overall take: Ultimately, do you think your book works as a book? How sure are you? (It's OK to be unsure.)

We'll revisit this question about how your book works as a book in various ways throughout the exercises to come, but for now, simply make sure you have an idea that requires a book.

## DEBRIEF, SUPPORT, AND TROUBLESHOOTING

Congratulations! You've taken the first step toward greater clarity about your book. Take a moment to reflect: How does it feel to have finished the activities in the first chapter?

For some authors, these exercises catalyze new insights and greater confidence about the project. They report with excitement:

> "I can identify my book's argument more clearly. I feel more confident about it!"

> "It actually pushed me to feel confident about actual, practical decisions about my book."

For others, though, these exercises prove challenging, raising questions and doubts:

> "Answering those hard questions about what my book actually is, questions that you can so easily avoid in just writing around things or making large claims [was a big challenge]."

> "[I was forced to confront] the feeling there are important topics I am excluding from the book, but cannot cover."

> "I felt like I was continuing to move in circles and still not knowing how to position the evidence or the argument."

It's totally normal to experience all of these feelings—especially doubt and uncertainty—at the end of each set of exercises.

Remember that this workbook is iterative. Not only will you revisit this activity in chapter 11, but you'll revise and refine your answers about your book's main claim in chapters 2–5. For now, work until you reach 80 percent confidence in your answers (Practice 2: "Put Progress over Perfection"), capture your doubts and questions (Practice 3: "Reflect Intentionally and Capture Doubts"), and forge ahead with the curriculum (Practice 1: "Prioritize Action").

Use the prompt below to capture these victories—small and large—and nagging doubts so that you can move on to the next chapter.

| | |
|---|---|
| How did this chapter's exercises give you new insights into your project? | |
| What questions or concerns not found in the list above do you now have about your book? | |
| What might you need to think more about as you go along? Which, if any, choices would you like to revisit later? | |

## CHAPTER 2

# Reviewing Your Book's Organizing Principle

## WHAT TO EXPECT

In the previous chapter, you learned that your scope and claims depend on the evidence you mobilize. You also assessed whether these dimensions of your book were well aligned and whether you might need to narrow your scope or add evidence to your book.

Just as scope, claims, and evidence are interdependent, so too are your book's structure and claims. Specifically, certain claims imply certain *organizing principles*—the term we use to describe the logic that explains how your chapters-as-units work in the book—and vice versa. In this chapter, you will consider your book's current structure and ask how well it serves your book's claims and scope.

### Time Investment

Expect to spend **about 3 hours** on this chapter's exercises. **Do not spend more than 4 hours** on them.

### Common Discoveries in Chapter 2

- **Your book has an organizing principle and you're able to name it**. Many dissertations are highly chapter-centric. You likely planned chapters that seemed to work well, but you never explicitly described how they're alike. In this chapter, you'll name your book's organizing principle. As one author put it: "I loved [these exercises] because it named a process of organization I intuitively knew I needed to do but did not have the language and examples to do."
- **You have multiple potential organizing principles**. When you were initially developing the project, you might not have considered that certain organizing principles work best to support certain types of claims. As a result, you might have settled on one or several loose organizing principles without ever intentionally evaluating them.
- **You can think about what is best for the book, *on its own terms***. You might have tried to do abstract work to restructure your book in the past, but struggled to think outside a chapter-centric framework. Many authors report that the sequencing of this workbook's early chapters gives them an unprecedented view of the book as a unified whole.
- **Your book *could* be many books, and you get to choose which one you want to write**. The organizing principle exercises in this chapter show you, concretely, that there is no one objectively right way to tell your book's story. Instead, certain structures do a better job than others of foregrounding certain claims.

- **You made decisions at an earlier stage without fully recognizing their implications**. Much of this workbook asks you to probe your book project from different angles and consider alternatives. As a result, it challenges you to imagine how different decisions would result in a slightly different book. Doing this work on your organizing principle can reveal that your book reflects many other decisions you made without realizing they were decisions or considering their impact on the book. Now, at the book stage, you're in the driver's seat: you get to choose how to structure your book to maximize its claims and narrative arc.

## Common Stumbling Blocks

- **An impulse to abandon the dissertation's organizing principle just to increase your book's chances of publication**. Many authors of books based on dissertations worry that editors will automatically reject books that are "too similar" (in terms of content or structure) to their dissertation forebears. Please don't let this fear drive you to consider—much less commit to!—a radically different organizing principle just for the sake of making your book visibly different from your dissertation. Remember, you're evaluating your book on its own terms; choose the organizing principle that best supports your book's claims.
- **Fear of commitment, lingering questions about the book's structure, or a desire to nail everything down before proceeding**. These mental hurdles seem to be opposites, but their root cause is the same: a general sense of unease, whether about the "permanence" of an organizing principle or about how it will play out in concrete terms at the chapter level. Luckily, our advice in both cases is the same: remember that this work is iterative and that you'll have plenty of opportunities to test how well this organizing principle works.
- **Inability to settle on an organizing principle**. If you don't have draft writing in some form to serve as the basis for at least half of the book's body chapters (including dissertation chapters, conference papers, journal articles, and rough writing and notes), you likely can't know yet which organizing principle will best serve your claims. If that's the case, you can use this activity proactively to identify several possible organizing principles instead of settling on just one.

## EXERCISES

### Step 1: Recognizing Organizing Principles

In the previous chapter, you learned how your book's scope and claims depend on the evidence you plan to offer your reader. You also assessed whether these dimensions of your book were well aligned, or whether you might need to narrow your scope or add evidence to your book.

In the same way that scope, claims, and evidence are interdependent, your book's structure supports certain claims better than others. Likewise, certain claims imply certain organizing principles. (You'll soon learn that your book's organization is a key piece of its argument.) In this chapter, you'll review and refine your book's structure, or plan a new structure that aligns better with your claim and scope.

But books sometimes have multiple potential organizing principles—that is, multiple major things that change from chapter to chapter. To see how this works, let's consider a sample book.

*Literary Studies*

Topic: Shifting notions of the concept of "family" as articulated in Francophone West and Central African literature

Chapter 1: The importance of lineage and genealogy in West African fables, epic tales, and griot songs that straddle the precolonial/colonial divide

Chapter 2: Heritage, genealogy, and childhood against the backdrop of colonization in Camara Laye's *L'enfant noir*

Chapter 3: Female experiences (motherhood, spousal duties) of family in Mariama Bâ's autobiographical epistolary novel *Une si longue lettre*

Chapter 4: Families in absurdist anti-colonial plays: Sony Lab'ou Tansi's *La parenthèse de sang* and *Moi, veuve de l'empire* (broken families)

Chapter 5: Postcolonial family and extended friendship networks in Marguerite Abouet's graphic novel *Aya de Yopougon*

Now ask yourself: In this sample book, what changes from chapter to chapter? To put it differently, fill in the blank: each chapter explores a different _____.

We noticed that this book has several potential organizing principles. When we outlined what changes from chapter to chapter, we identified three main elements:

- **Chronological period**: We move forward in time from the precolonial period (chapter 1) to the colonial period (chapter 2), and on to three points in the postcolonial period (chapters 3–5).
- **Genre**: Each chapter considers a different literary genre: written accounts of oral storytelling (chapter 1), a novel (chapter 2), an epistolary novel (chapter 3), theater (chapter 4), and graphic novels (chapter 5).
- **Author**: Each chapter after the first centers on literature by one main author: Camara Laye (chapter 2), Mariama Bâ (chapter 3), Sony Lab'ou Tansi (chapter 4), and Marguerite Abouet (chapter 5).

That's a lot of change. What kind of story, you may wonder, is this book telling? Is it a story about how notions of family changed over time in Francophone West and Central African literature? Or is it about how notions of family changed across genres? Or about how different West and Central African authors represented the family? We don't know. But you can probably intuit that if the book is going to tell a streamlined, cohesive story, it will need to prioritize one of the organizing principles.

To figure out which one is (or should be) the *main* organizing principle, this author should identify the question that each principle implies. Then she can assess whether the evidence she presents in each chapter allows her to answer that question.

Let's see how this would look:

| Organizing principle: | Chronological period |
|---|---|
| Question this organizing principle implies: | How did understandings of family in Francophone West and Central African literature shift over time? |

Now reflect on whether you think her evidence allows her to answer this question. Is this book well or ill equipped to answer this *chronological* question? Why/how so?

While we think this book is invested in examining change over time, notice that each chapter focuses on only one (or at most a few) works by one author. We're curious about whether such a narrow focus allows the book's author to make broad generalizations about change over time. Is one work by one author really illustrative of a whole period? We aren't convinced.

We think this book would need to broaden its evidence base to make well-supported chronological claims. Furthermore, if this book's main organizing principle were chronological period, we would expect each chapter to center on a readily recognizable historical moment ("first contact," major anti-colonial struggles, independence, etc.).

As a result, we would characterize chronological period as a *secondary organizing principle* in this book. In fact, many books have chronology as a secondary organizing principle.

Let's move on to another organizing principle.

| Organizing principle: | Literary genre |
|---|---|
| Question this organizing principle implies: | How do different literary genres allow different notions of "family" to crystallize in Francophone West and Central African literature? |

Reflect on whether you think her evidence allows her to answer this question. Is her book well or ill equipped to answer this *genre-focused* question? Why/how so?

Again, we wonder whether one author (and sometimes just one work!) is enough evidence to support broad claims about literary genres. If genre were truly the organizing principle, we would expect the fourth chapter, for instance, to include plays by many more playwrights.

Note, too, that this organizing principle would mean that this author's main question is different from the one she seems most interested in answering. The chapter descriptions suggest an interest in themes related to families. But the genre-focused organizing principle would require the book to make more prominent formal and aesthetic arguments. Instead of asking how works/authors represent changing notions of family, it would likely focus on the aesthetic and generic possibilities offered by each literary form for developing notions of family.

Consequently, we would characterize genre as a *major book thread* (you will learn more about these in chapter 11) but not as the book's organizing principle.

Finally, let's consider "author" as an organizing principle:

| Organizing principle: | Author |
|---|---|
| Question this organizing principle implies: | How do different Francophone West and Central African authors express changing notions of "family"? |

Reflect: Does each of this author's chapters allow her to answer this question? This time, the answer (except for the first chapter, which we'll discuss soon) is a resounding *yes*.

Before committing to this structure, the author would want to make sure this is a question she's interested in answering. If she were more interested in answering the genre-focused question, she could certainly do so. However, such a major shift in her book's organizing principle and question would involve enormous amounts of new research and could take years to complete. If you're on the tenure track or need your book to appear within the next three and a half years, we recommend that you avoid changes that would involve significant volumes of new research.

We also want to point out that merely identifying an author-centric organizing principle does *not* absolve the author of having to carefully select and justify the authors she includes in her study. She can't just assume that as long as each chapter centers on one author, the book is cohesive. She'll have to explain why these authors (of all the authors she could have chosen) allow her to teach the book's key lessons. We'll guide you to do this work in chapter 6.

Finally, note that her first chapter falls outside the author-centric schema. This is perfectly fine. Many books have a first body chapter that does not fit neatly within the rest of their book's organizing principle (Katelyn's book included!). We call these chapters "background/historical" chapters—those that present information outside the book's main evidence base that establishes information on which later chapters will depend. Sometimes such a chapter presents conceptual information that other chapters go on to apply to specific cases. If you have a "background/historical" chapter, there's no need to try to force it into your organizing principle.

A final note on organizing principles: editors will sometimes consider your project's organizing principle (without necessarily using that term) when assessing the potential for individual chapters to be adopted in courses. For instance, an author-centric organizing principle can make certain chapters strong candidates for required or recommended reading in undergraduate or graduate course sessions focusing on that author. A media-centric organizing principle can make some chapters useful for other courses. If you're hesitating between two organizing principles, think about whether one of them would make your chapters more suitable to assign as standalone readings.

---

*Want Additional Practice?*

Identify the organizing principle of your model book(s).

---

## Step 2: Identifying Your Book's Current Primary Organizing Principle

Now you're going to apply the same ideas to your own book project. What underlying organizing principle currently unites your book's chapters? Alternatively, finish this sentence: "Each chapter explores a different . . ." For now, if you have multiple potential organizing principles, choose the one that seems to be the main driver of your book's logic.

You'll complete these tables in multiple steps. Right now you're in step 2 of the chapter, so fill in only the "Step 2" box in the first table. Step 3 will guide you to fill in the "Step 3" boxes, step 4 the "Step 4" boxes, and so on. Note that step 5 has three sub-steps (A–C).

| Step 2: My book's organizing principle: | |
|---|---|
| | |

| Step 4: Question this organizing principle implies: | | | |
|---|---|---|---|
| Step 5A: My book is ___ to answer this question. | ☐ Well equipped | | ☐ Ill equipped |
| Step 5B: Justify your answer to step 5A. | | | |
| Step 5C: Ultimately, this is . . . | ☐ My book's primary organizing principle | ☐ My book's secondary organizing principle | ☐ A major book thread |

| Step 3: My book's *main question* (from chapter 1): | | | |
|---|---|---|---|
| Step 4: *Organizing principle* this question implies: | | | |
| Note: If the "organizing principle this question implies" is the same as the organizing principle you wrote in step 2 of table 1, you don't have to fill out the rest of this table. | | | |
| Step 5A: My book is ___ to answer this question. | ☐ Well equipped | | ☐ Ill equipped |
| Step 5B: Justify your answer to step 5A. | | | |
| Step 5C: Ultimately, this is . . . | ☐ My book's primary organizing principle | ☐ My book's secondary organizing principle | ☐ A major book thread |

| Step 3: Alternative possible organizing principle: | | |
|---|---|---|
| Step 4: Question this organizing principle implies: | | |
| Step 5A: My book is ___ to answer this question. | ☐ Well equipped | ☐ Ill equipped |

| Step 5B: Justify your answer to step 5A. | | | |
|---|---|---|---|
| Step 5C: Ultimately, this is . . . | ☐ My book's primary organizing principle | ☐ My book's secondary organizing principle | ☐ A major book thread |

| Step 3: Alternative possible organizing principle: | | | |
|---|---|---|---|
| Step 4: Question this organizing principle implies: | | | |
| Step 5A: My book is ___ to answer this question. | ☐ Well equipped | | ☐ Ill equipped |
| Step 5B: Justify your answer to step 5A. | | | |
| Step 5C: Ultimately, this is . . . | ☐ My book's primary organizing principle | ☐ My book's secondary organizing principle | ☐ A major book thread |

| Step 3: Alternative possible organizing principle: | | | |
|---|---|---|---|
| Step 4: Question this organizing principle implies: | | | |
| Step 5A: My book is ___ to answer this question. | ☐ Well equipped | | ☐ Ill equipped |
| Step 5B: Justify your answer to step 5A. | | | |
| Step 5C: Ultimately, this is . . . | ☐ My book's primary organizing principle | ☐ My book's secondary organizing principle | ☐ A major book thread |

## Step 3: Imagining All of Your Book's Potential Organizing Principles

In this step, you'll lay out several additional organizing principles that could drive your book.

In this chapter, you're learning that your organizing principle and main book question are linked. In chapter 1, you produced a main book question. Now you'll work backward to generate an organizing principle from your book question. In the second table, write your question from chapter 1 in the first "Step 3" box. Then write down the organizing principle this question implies in the second "Step 3" box.

Finally, in the "Step 3" box of the remaining tables, imagine other possible organizing principles that *could* animate your book. Review the list below to generate ideas. Don't worry if you leave one or more tables blank.

Common organizing principles include:

- Chronological period
- Author/person/group/organization/administrative unit
- Genre/medium
- Work
- Outlet (*Time* magazine vs. *New York Times* vs. *Forbes*)
- Geographical context/nation/region/city
- Type of _____ (e.g., type of liberty: chapter 1 on physical liberty, chapter 2 on psychological liberty, chapter 3 on metaphysical liberty; type of network: chapter 1 on open networks, chapter 2 on closed networks, chapter 3 on permeable networks, etc.)
- Idea/concept/theme (e.g., chapter 1 on love, chapter 2 on beauty, chapter 3 on the body)
- Scale (individual vs. family vs. community vs. city vs. state vs. nation)

## Step 4: Stating the Implied Questions

In the tables you began in the previous step, lay out the question that each organizing principle implies. For inspiration, you can return to the introductory material on the book about families in Francophone West and Central African fiction.

## Step 5: Choosing Your Organizing Principle

Now complete the remainder of the tables—step 5 boxes A through C—to identify how well equipped your book is to answer the question implied by each organizing principle. Based on your answer, identify your book's main organizing principle, secondary organizing principle (if any; usually chronology, but also anything that can easily be ordered from "most" to "least" or vice versa), and/or main threads by reflecting on your chapters' ability to answer these potential questions.

Note: Remember that your book's main idea and organization are linked. Consequently, you'll be using your organizing principle's implied question as the starting point for articulating your book's main idea in later chapters. If you aren't yet fully satisfied that your book's core work is asking and answering that question, you can use the exercises in appendix C to explore alternatives based on your topic (produced in chapter 1).

## Step 6: Reflecting on Your Organizing Principle

Reflect on the relationship between your book's current organizing principle and the organizing principle implied by the question your book is best equipped to answer.

<table>
<tr><td>How much has your organizing principle changed? How confident do you feel about the new organizing principle, if you have one? What evidence will you need to support the new organizing principle?</td><td></td></tr>
</table>

## *SORTING CHECKPOINT*

If your organizing principle has not changed, proceed.

If your organizing principle will change between the dissertation and the book, *make sure it fits the evidence you have now*, especially if you're on the tenure track and need a book. If you have the evidence, proceed. If you need to completely redo the book's organizing principle *and* its evidence base, this is probably not a book you have time to write on the tenure track (or before you land a tenure-track job), even with junior research leave. At this point, you must keep *either* your evidence base *or* your organizing principle. Decide whether your main priority is to add new evidence while keeping your current organizing principle or to rework the organizing principle but keep the evidence base. Then revise your answers to the questions in this chapter before proceeding.

## DEBRIEF, SUPPORT, AND TROUBLESHOOTING

Here are some common thoughts, challenges, and questions that authors report having at the end of this chapter's work. Check the ones that apply to you, read the advice below (feel free to skip whatever doesn't apply), and then proceed to the debrief prompt.

- ☐ **I'm torn between two primary organizing principles.**
  This workbook is iterative, and you'll revisit your decisions later. For now, commit to the main organizing principle that you currently believe works best.
- ☐ **I think I have more than one secondary organizing principle.**
  That's fine. In the chapters to come, you might discover that one of your two secondary organizing principles is more important than the other. Or you might find that your secondary organizing principles are interconnected. And in chapter 8, you'll learn new ways to think about how your book's organization develops. For now, though, try to identify no more than *two* (at most) secondary organizing principles.
- ☐ **What if I've decided that my book's organizing principle will be very different from that of my dissertation?**
  Great! Often PhD candidates put together (with the help of their committee) a project centered on coherent chapters, each related to the overarching project. Before you completed your PhD research, you may have had only a vague idea of your project's main claims. Because claims and structure go hand in hand, your dissertation's organizing principle might have been ill suited to the claims you're now interested in making. Keep in mind, though, that restructuring your analyses to support a new organizing principle can be a lot of work. If you're already on a tight timeline, proceed with caution.

☐ **Can I change my organizing principle later?**

Yes. Some (but not many) authors discover later (usually around chapters 4–5 or chapters 9–10) that a different organizing principle is better suited to their book's claims. Now that you've completed the exercises once, you should have a good sense of what you'll need to consider regarding your book's organizing principle and claims. If you must change your organizing principle later, the decision will likely be easier.

☐ **I realized that I have a chronological organizing principle, but there are gaps.**

No book can cover all moments equally, and slight gaps or overlaps, if they're justifiable, are usually fine. In chapter 7, you will learn new ways to assess this dimension of your project.

☐ **Can I use the concept of "organizing principles" in other academic writing?**

Yes! The concept of an organizing principle can be useful for mapping out the sections of an article, for instance.

| | |
|---|---|
| How did this chapter's exercises give you new insights into your project? | |
| What questions or concerns not found in the list above do you now have about your book? | |
| What might you need to think more about as you go along? Which, if any, choices would you like to revisit later? | |

## CHAPTER 3

# Drafting Your First Book Question

## WHAT TO EXPECT

In chapter 2, you identified your book's main organizing principle and wrote down the question it implies. In this chapter and throughout the rest of the workbook, you'll use this question as a drafting and revising tool—it will help you toggle between your book's main ideas and the evidence in your chapters, and it will eventually be reframed as part of the book argument. You'll also stress-test this question to make sure it captures your book's central actors and actions.

### Time Investment

Expect to spend **about 2 hours** on the exercises in this chapter. **Do not spend more than 3 hours** on them.

### Common Discoveries in Chapter 3

- **Your book feels more tangible.** Chapters 3–5 and their chapter-level counterparts, chapters 9–10, are the crux of this work because they ask you to commit to your main book- and chapter-level takeaways. Consequently, many authors find that the exercises in chapter 3, while challenging, mark the first time they can concretely see their book's main work.

- **In descriptions of the book (job and fellowship applications, book abstract), you've been trying to describe the book using too many "big concepts," believing you could cover all of them.** The length of academic books (typically 80–100K words, though this varies by field) deceives many authors into believing they will have the space to develop any interesting thread they want. Sure, you *could* do so, but your reader would likely leave with merely a collection of interesting insights rather than a coherent takeaway.

- **You've been interested in _____ all along.** Book questions are limiting and reductive by design. Stripping away extraneous information and distilling your book's main question forces clarity. You might arrive at this insight when you first articulate your book question and think "Yes! That's what I've been doing all along! It seems simple, but that's the core of what I'm doing!" Or you might reach it by putting something down that you sense is "not quite right" and exploring why you have this impression. Many authors discover, for instance, that they'd been presenting their book's work with the wrong actor at its core or that they'd been using a not-quite-right term to describe their book's main interest.

- **The chapters are supporting your book's argument—but you don't have the full picture yet**. In this chapter, you'll do some preliminary work to check whether the question you write is something that each chapter explicitly answers. Doing so will help you grasp the relationship between the book and its chapters.

## Common Stumbling Blocks

- **Feeling that your book question is limiting and reductive**. Reducing your book's main work to one apparently simple question can feel limiting. Try to think of it as prioritizing and distilling to ensure that the book's main ideas stay at the forefront of each chapter. Your book will certainly do much more interesting, insightful, and nuanced work than can be captured in its first book question. But for now, respect the limited genre.
- **Wondering whether this book question is rigorous enough**. Again, book questions are reductive by design. You'll revise your book questions in future chapters, but for now, simpler is better. You learned in chapter 1 that first books make claims about the evidence base, event(s), places, or case studies they consider. Your first book question merely points to your book's most important lesson about this topic.
- **Wanting to write a very broad question**. It's common to think your book needs to answer a big, important question, maybe something along the lines of "What is the meaning of X?" Questions like that may point to the significance of your book project. But in this workbook, we're going to insist that you write a question *you can actually answer*—thoroughly, specifically, and with variations across your chapters. So don't worry if your question seems narrow, boring, or obvious for now. You'll have plenty of time to address the significance later.

## EXERCISES

### Step 1: Understanding Book Questions

It can be helpful to think of your book as an intellectual tour and yourself as a tour guide. Imagine a tour guide who assembles the tour group at a large statue of a sunbonnet-wearing woman who carries a baby and grips a rifle with her other hand. "Look at this statue," the tour guide begins. "What kind of woman is it asking us to remember?"[1]

The members of the tour group tilt their heads to look up. They stare at the statue. They're hooked—and they're going to listen to whatever the tour guide says next.

Similarly, when you take your readers on an intellectual tour, you can ask them to pay attention to evidence with questions in mind. Clear questions focus your readers' attention. And questions that direct that attention to your objects of study—your texts, images, research subjects, historical figures, and so on—are the most useful, because you'll be able to walk your readers through the answers.

Even more importantly for our purposes, questions can serve as drafting and revising tools. They focus *your* attention and help you prioritize your most important ideas. In this chapter, you'll settle on what we call your first "book question," or a central question that your book will answer. (In chapter 4, you'll write one or two additional questions.) The key thing to know about this book question is that we're asking you to answer it *in every chapter of your book*. Furthermore, each chapter will give a *slightly different answer to the question*.

Consider the following book question and the corresponding chapter answers:

**Book question:** In the twenty-first-century United States, how do various types of children's picture books by Black authors communicate anti-racist lessons?

**Chapter 1 answer:** Biographies of famous Black people highlight individual resilience in the face of racism and counter White-centric history by raising awareness of their protagonists' accomplishments.

**Chapter 2 answer:** Fiction about Black children that doesn't mention racism emphasizes that all children deserve to be celebrated in narratives featuring joy, tenderness, and/or family/community bonds.

**Chapter 3 answer:** Nonfiction books that teach explicit lessons about race, racism, and activism seek to explain social phenomena and communicate that individuals can make a positive difference.

**Chapter 4 answer:** Fiction about children facing episodes of racism emphasizes that racism is wrong and illustrates ways children and those around them can affirm their individual worth and dignity.

**Chapter 5 answer:** Fiction that explicitly affirms Black identity, culture, and/or appearance communicates that its protagonists are valuable just the way they are and/or that they belong to a strong and admirable community.

Note that the question is about the book's objects of study: children's picture books that communicate anti-racist lessons. Each chapter contributes a different answer to the question. Each chapter, in other words, adds a new layer to our understanding of the types of books that convey anti-racist lessons and what those lessons are. After reading this book, the readers should have a good understanding of the range of anti-racist children's literature that circulated in this time and place.

We start with book questions—and spend a lot of time on them!—because using them simplifies the process of envisioning the book as a whole. If your book began as a dissertation, it may be challenging to view your manuscript this way. Both of us (Katelyn and Allison) started our dissertations with our respective topics in mind, and then we wrote one chapter, and then another chapter, and so on until we finished. We made sure each chapter was organized around an argument, but we didn't fully grasp what arguments our dissertations *as a whole* were making until the very end. As a result, the best-argued units of our dissertations were the chapters. But solid scholarly books can't just enumerate many interesting things that eventually add up to something. Instead, they start with clearly identified claims and carefully deploy evidence and sub-arguments to support them. By using our "book questions/chapter answers" framework, you'll figure out how to align your book's key ideas with the evidence you analyze in the chapters.

Before you draft your first book question, let's consider why it's important for the book question to be answered in *every* chapter (with the exception of the introduction, the conclusion, and any background/historical or conceptual chapters). Imagine that your book is a course that you're teaching or taking. Typically, a course has several well-defined learning outcomes or objectives, centered on the content knowledge and skills the students should have acquired by the end of the course. For example, a course might have the following objective: "By the end of the course, you will be able to describe how identity is conceived in different ways across the Francophone world." It's unlikely that this course would have just one unit on identity, with the other units covering totally different topics. Instead, each unit would likely focus on a different facet of identity, or identity in a different region of the Francophone world. In a well-designed course, each unit advances every one of the course's main objectives.

The same principle applies if your book is the course, your book questions are the objectives, and your chapters are the units. Each book question should point to a piece of knowledge that is taught—with variations—in each chapter. It may be tempting to write one book question that refers to what you teach in chapter 1, another book question that refers to what you teach in chapter 2, and so on. Resist this temptation! Instead, the "lesson" of Book Question 1 should be taught in chapter 1, and then in a slightly different form in chapter 2, and in yet another form in chapter 3. Draft a question that captures what's going on in the book as a whole—an idea that each chapter will develop. If this seems hard, don't worry! We'll help you get there.

Finally, keep in mind that the book question format is restrictive by design. Drafting these questions involves hierarchizing, streamlining, and deciding what matters most in your book. That's not to say there won't be other interesting threads. There will be. It's just that those threads won't be central to your book.

## Step 2: Stress-Testing the Actors and Actions of Your Book Question

Good news: you already have a book question! You drafted it in chapter 2 of this workbook, when you settled on an organizing principle that implies a main question.

In chapter 1, we asked you to quickly consider the alignment between your book's main claim, question, and evidence, which involved considering what the evidence implies about your book's main actor. But when you produced your organizing principle question in chapter 2, we didn't ask you to think critically about the content, language, or structure of your organizing principle's implied question. In this exercise, you'll make sure this question contains a subject, a verb, and possibly a direct object that clearly reflect your book's main story. Consider the following examples:

**HISTORY**

| Question my organizing principle implies (emerging Book Question 1): | What international organizations facilitated the second wave of emigration from the Eastern Bloc, 1986–1987? |
|---|---|
| **Actor** in my organizing principle's question: | International organizations |
| Notes on actor—is this *actually* what I study in my book? Do I have the evidence to support an extended analysis of this actor? Are any important actors missing? | Yes, this is what I actually study. Each chapter looks at a different organization. But I do notice that the *people* themselves are absent. They've always been an important secondary actor. I wonder how or where I can represent them. |
| **Action** in my organizing principle's question: | Facilitated |
| Notes on action—is this *actually* what I study in my book? | Yes, I think this is right. The second wave was not *created* by the international organizations, but they were a major actor. |

| Direct object or effect(s) in my organizing principle's question: | The second wave of emigration |
|---|---|
| Notes on object or effects—is this *actually* what I show in my book? | Yes, I think this is right, too. An alternative could be "emigrants' escape from . . . ," which would center the people more. But I think the wave is an important idea. |
| Revised question (if necessary): | I'm going to keep my question the same for now. |

Note: If you completed the work in appendix C because you weren't sure that your organizing principle's implied question truly reflected the work at the heart of your book, use the claim you produced in those exercises instead of your organizing principle's implied question.

This organizing principle's question seems well suited to a book-length story. The author will want to ensure that they intend *international organizations* (and not, say, emigrants or another actor) to be the book's main actor. They should also ask themselves whether *facilitated* is the main action their book studies. In the next activity, the author will scrutinize the question word (here: *what*) to ask whether they are most interested in telling a *what*, a *how*, or a *why* story.

## LITERARY STUDIES

| Question my organizing principle implies (emerging Book Question 1): | How do different Francophone West and Central African authors express changing notions of "family"? |
|---|---|
| **Actor** in my organizing principle's question: | West and Central African authors |
| Notes on actor—is this *actually* what I study in my book? Do I have the evidence to support an extended analysis of this actor? Are any important actors missing? | Yes, I think this is right. I'm wondering, though, if "texts" or "representations" are actually what I study. How do different textual representations testify to changing notions of "family"? I guess I will need to think more about whether the paradigm I develop is tied to the author (am I, for instance, proposing that [Author A] develops their own notion of family that's distinct from that of [Author B])? |
| **Action** in my organizing principle's question: | Express |
| Notes on action—is this *actually* what I study in my book? | Yes, I think this is right. Alternatives would be "create" or "represent." I think represent is more appropriate than create. |
| **Direct object** or **effect(s)** in my organizing principle's question: | Changing notions of "family" |
| Notes on object or effects—is this *actually* what I show in my book? | Yes, I think this is right, too, but now a question that I have is whether this grammatical direct object is actually the subject of my book. Should I rewrite the sentence to center it (and not authors)? Something like "What changing notions of 'family' emerge in West and Central African fiction?" |
| Revised question (if necessary): | What changing notions of "family" emerge in fictional works by Francophone West and Central African authors? |

This organizing principle's question seems well suited to a book-length story. The author will want to ensure that she intends *authors* (and not, say, works, familial roles, or notions of family) to be the main actor. She should also ask herself whether *express* is the main action her book studies. In the next activity, the author will scrutinize the question word (here: *how*) to ask whether she is most interested in telling a *what*, a *how*, or a *why* story.

## SOCIOLOGY

| | |
|---|---|
| Question my organizing principle implies (emerging Book Question 1): | How did queer Québécois nightlife change over time? |
| **Actor** in my organizing principle's question: | Queer Québécois nightlife |
| Notes on actor—is this *actually* what I study in my book? Do I have the evidence to support an extended analysis of this actor? Are any important actors missing? | Yes, this is definitely a main thing I study in my book. I notice, though, that the other main thing I study (the *révolution tranquille*) is missing. Shouldn't it be in this main question? |
| **Action** in my organizing principle's question: | Change |
| Notes on action—is this *actually* what I study in my book? | Yes, I mean technically that's right. But it seems like if I'm writing a question tying my two main concepts together, then I will need a different verb. |
| **Direct object** or **effect(s)** in my organizing principle's question: | There is no direct object. |
| Notes on object or effects—is this *actually* what I show in my book? | Maybe adding in an object would help me tie these two concepts together. Am I studying legacies of the *révolution tranquille* in queer Québécois nightlife? How queer Québécois nightlife testifies to the *révolution tranquille*? |
| Revised question (if necessary): | I think a better question would be: How did the legacies of the *révolution tranquille* translate into changes in queer Québécois nightlife from 1973 to the present? |

This organizing principle's question could be well suited to a book-length story; however, the author noticed that one of their main concepts was missing and that there was no direct object or verb beyond "change." They rightly asked whether they could reformulate their emerging Book Question 1 to tie these two concepts together and worked to do so. Since the revised question is quite different from their original question, they should redo this step's work on the revised question to make sure it captures what they mean to say at the book level.

For instance, we could imagine the following alternative questions working well for their book project. Notice how answering each question would result in a slightly different story.

- How do changes in queer Québécois nightlife from 1973 to the present testify to the lasting legacies of the *révolution tranquille*? (Notice that the time frame captures the change over time; here, changes in queer Québécois nightlife becomes the main actor.)

- How did queer Québécois nightclub-goers refashion the nightlife scene from 1973 to the present? (Notice that the time frame captures the change over time; here, the nightclub-goers are the actors who are actively refashioning the scene.)
- How did queer Québécois nightclub-goers develop what I call [term] from 1973 to the present? (Notice that the time frame captures the change over time; here, the nightclub-goers are the actors who are developing the key term.)

Now it's your turn. Complete the table to assess your organizing principle's question and turn it into Book Question 1.

| | |
|---|---|
| Question my organizing principle implies (emerging Book Question 1): | |
| **Actor** in my organizing principle's question: | |
| Notes on actor—is this *actually* what I study in my book? Do I have the evidence to support an extended analysis of this actor? Are any important actors missing? | |
| **Action** in my organizing principle's question: | |
| Notes on action—is this *actually* what I study in my book? | |
| **Direct object** or **effect(s)** in my organizing principle's question: | |
| Notes on object or effects—is this *actually* what I show in my book? | |
| Revised question (if necessary): | |

## Step 3: Revising Your Question Word

Our main goal in this chapter is to produce one big question to which each chapter offers an answer. In step 2, you stress-tested the structure of the question by probing its actor(s), action(s), and directionality. In this step, you'll probe another critical component of your book question: the interrogative word with which it begins.

The question word in your book question determines the corresponding chapter-level answers. In this step, you'll brainstorm many ways of formulating your book question—using different interrogative words—to decide which one truly captures your book's investments.

First, read through the following series of *what*, *how*, and *why* questions.

### HISTORY

| | |
|---|---|
| Revised Book Question 1 (as a question): | How did **international organizations** facilitate the second wave of emigration from the Eastern Bloc, 1986–1987? |
| **What** questions my book could ask: | • What **international organizations** facilitated the second wave of emigration from the Eastern Bloc, 1986–1987?<br>• What **activities by international organizations** facilitated the second wave of emigration from the Eastern Bloc, 1986–1987?<br>• What **characteristics of international organizations** facilitated the second wave of emigration from the Eastern Bloc, 1986–1987?<br>• What factors caused **international organizations** to facilitate the second wave of emigration from the Eastern Bloc, 1986–1987? |
| **How** questions my book could ask: | • How did **international organizations** facilitate the second wave of emigration from the Eastern Bloc, 1986–1987?<br>• How did **emigrants** navigate **international organizations** facilitating the second wave of emigration from the Eastern Bloc, 1986–1987? |
| **Why** questions my book could ask: | • Why did **international organizations** facilitate the second wave of emigration from the Eastern Bloc, 1986–1987? |

### LITERARY STUDIES

| | |
|---|---|
| Revised Book Question 1 (as a question): | What **innovative literary styles** did twentieth-century Scandinavian novelists develop? |
| **What** questions my book could ask: | • What are the **key features** of twentieth-century Scandinavian novelists' **innovative literary styles**?<br>• What twentieth-century Scandinavian novelists developed **innovative literary styles**?<br>• What **works** exemplify twentieth-century Scandinavian literary experimentation? |
| **How** questions my book could ask: | • How did **innovative literary styles** develop in twentieth-century Scandinavia?<br>• How did **twentieth-century Scandinavian novelists** develop innovative literary styles?<br>• How did **twentieth-century Scandinavian innovative literary styles** build on or depart from other innovative literary styles of the time? |
| **Why** questions my book could ask: | • Why did **twentieth-century Scandinavian novelists** experiment with form to develop innovative literary styles?<br>• Why did **twentieth-century Scandinavian innovative literary styles** take the forms they did? |

**POLITICAL SCIENCE**

| Revised Book Question 1 (as a question): | To what degrees and in what ways do **BIPOC mayors** represent minority interests? |
|---|---|
| **What** questions my book could ask: | • What factors do **BIPOC mayors** consider when representing minority interests?<br>• What **factors** make some **BIPOC mayors** more likely than others to represent minority interests?<br>• What **actions** illustrate **BIPOC mayors'** ways of representing minority interests?<br>• What **BIPOC mayors** represent minority interests? |
| **How** questions my book could ask: | • How do **BIPOC mayors** represent minority interests?<br>• How successful are **BIPOC mayors'** efforts to represent minority interests?<br>• How do **BIPOC mayors** understand their own responsibilities with respect to the various communities they represent?<br>• How do **BIPOC mayors** navigate competing interests from various constituents, including minority groups?<br>• How do **various groups** expect **BIPOC mayors** to act and to what degree/under what conditions do they adhere to these expectations? |
| **Why** questions my book could ask: | • Why do **BIPOC mayors** represent minority interests?<br>• Why might **BIPOC mayors** be expected to represent communities in ways their non-BIPOC peers are not? |

Now it's your turn. Use the examples to draft a variety of what, how, and why questions that your book *could* ask.

| Revised Book Question 1 (as a question): | |
|---|---|
| **What** questions my book could ask: | |

| **How** questions my book could ask: | |
|---|---|
| **Why** questions my book could ask: | |

## Step 4: Checking Your Book Question Candidates against Your Chapters

When you were producing the what, how, and why questions, you likely noticed a few that best capture the intellectual tour that you'll give in your book.

If you had very strong feelings about *one* emerging book question in particular, use it here. If you haven't yet settled on your top question, use *up to three* for this activity.

Later in this workbook, you'll see how the book questions function as a point of dialogue between the book level and the chapter level. In chapters 9–10, you'll develop sets of chapter answers to the book questions. At this stage, it's important to make sure that your book questions will actually work as book questions for the purposes of these exercises. We don't want you to spend time refining book questions that will make you tear your hair out in chapters 9–10.

In the table that follows, write down what you think your book question will be. Then imagine that the *only thing each chapter could do was directly answer this question*. What would the chapter-specific answers sound like? Write a template for the answers. Don't answer the question at this point—just write a template with brackets for the chapter-specific parts.

If you can think of other possible questions, repeat the process.

| Book Question 1: | What **innovative literary styles** did twentieth-century Scandinavian novelists develop? |
|---|---|
| Answer Template (each chapter responds directly): | [This/these chapter-specific Scandinavian novelists] developed a style known as [chapter-specific innovative literary style]. |

| Alternative Book Question 1: | What are the **key features** of twentieth-century Scandinavian novelists' **innovative literary styles**? |
|---|---|
| Answer Template (each chapter responds directly): | The key features of [this chapter-specific innovative literary style] are [chapter-specific features]. |

| Alternative Book Question 1: | How did **twentieth-century Scandinavian innovative literary styles** build on or depart from other innovative literary styles of the time? |
|---|---|
| Answer Template (each chapter responds directly): | [This chapter-specific innovative literary style] [built on or departed from other literary styles of the time in this chapter-specific way]. |

| Book Question 1: | |
|---|---|
| Answer Template (each chapter responds directly): | |

| Alternative Book Question 1: | |
|---|---|
| Answer Template (each chapter responds directly): | |

Then, to make sure your templates will work, think about how you would replace the brackets with phrases specific to each of your book's body chapters. (As always, you can exclude any introductory or background/historical chapters.) Don't spend much time on this, and don't write the answers down unless you want to; just mentally test your templates to get a sense for whether they can answer the book question. This work will likely feel similar to the work you did to identify your book's organizing principle.

Note that in the example, the phrase "innovative literary styles" acts as a kind of verbal "bucket" that carries the specific literary styles discussed in the chapters. If you're stuck, circle your own "bucket concept." What smaller concepts does it hold? In the example, the smaller concepts might be Nordic noir, the Danish gothic, Scandinavian social realism, and so on.

After writing your templates and thinking through your chapter-level answers, you should have a better sense of *whether* your book question works well with your chapter-level material (and, if you were testing alternative book questions, *how* each differs—in ways large and small—from the others). You might have also discovered that your book is definitely *not* equipped to answer one or more of the possible book questions. For instance, you might have tested "Why did twentieth-century Scandinavian novelists experiment with form to develop innovative literary styles?" However, upon reflection, you realized that your book is not at all interested in answering (or even able to answer!) this causal question, which is beyond the scope of what you can answer using textual analysis.

If you did this exercise with several possible book questions, choose your top one. This will become your Book Question 1. Use the following checklist to double-check Book Question 1 before you commit to it.

- ☐ This is a question I can actually answer given the evidence I have or will have. (For instance, I'm not attempting to answer a historical question using fictional literature, or to answer a literary historical question with literary critical approaches.)
- ☐ Even if it feels somewhat basic in its current form, this is a question I actually want to ask at the book level and answer at the chapter level.
- ☐ Each chapter will offer an explicit, direct response to this question. (That is, it's not something I lay out explicitly in my book's introduction but only allude to in the chapters.)
- ☐ If I were speaking to an editor, this question would capture my book at its most fundamental level. It's what my book is *really* exploring.

Congratulations! You've written your first book question—a central question that the reader will be able to answer by the end of the book.

> **Want Additional Practice?**
>
> Identify the topic and central question of your model book(s). Then, if you want to, figure out how (or whether) each body chapter answers the question.

## DEBRIEF, SUPPORT, AND TROUBLESHOOTING

- ☐ **I think my first book question is too simple**.
  We get it! Some people find writing their first book question liberating because doing so establishes a tangible bar for their book's content. For them, drafting their first book question can begin to clarify what to cut and what to keep. But other authors

resist this limited, direct way of distilling their book project. If you're part of the latter group, please trust that this sometimes uncomfortable work will produce a stronger and more coherent book. It will also help you preemptively address the biggest problem acquisitions editors regularly see in book proposals by authors of first books: an inability to boil the book's main claims down to one sentence.

☐ **What will I do with the intellectual threads that don't fit into my first book question?**
Your book will do much more than answer your first book question. In chapter 4, you'll draft two additional book questions. Together, the book questions will form your book's core. But your book will also develop several threads—important discussions that weave throughout your book, but that may not be central to every chapter. You'll capture these threads in chapter 11.

☐ **My terminology isn't quite right.**
You might sense that your book question's terms aren't quite right—that they could benefit from minor tweaks. In chapters 5 and 10, you'll revise your work, so for now, record these reservations and move on. If, however, you believe your terminology might be fundamentally flawed (that is, it would benefit from systematic rethinking, rather than tweaking), see appendix D.

☐ **I'm struggling to pick between two main actors.**
Many authors study interrelated topics, actors, processes, or events, but have never forced themselves to choose one main actor and action. If you doubt that you've chosen your own book's main actor correctly, you're in good company. For now, pick the book question that seems *most right* to you and save the other one(s). If you conclude later on that a different formulation works better, you can always tweak or swap out your book question.

| | |
|---|---|
| How did this chapter's exercises give you new insights into your project? | |
| What questions or concerns not found in the list above do you now have about your book? | |

| What might you need to think more about as you go along? Which, if any, choices would you like to revisit later? | |

## CHAPTER 4

# Drafting Your Remaining Book Questions

## WHAT TO EXPECT

In this chapter, you'll write one or two additional book questions. Ideally, these questions will be spin-offs of the central question you drafted in chapter 3—they'll ask about the causes, results, processes, agents, contexts, or related concepts of Book Question 1. As you did in chapter 3, you'll stress-test the new questions to make sure they capture your book's actors and actions.

These two or three book questions will guide your book work. In chapter 9, you will explicitly articulate each core body chapter's answer to each book question. Ultimately, these book questions and their chapter-level counterparts will inform your chapter revisions (chapters 14–16) and help you identify what to cut.

### Time Investment

Expect to spend **about 2 hours** on this chapter's exercises. **Do not spend more than 4 hours** on them.

### Common Discoveries in Chapter 4

- **Your book feels more concrete than you thought it was—or maybe it just feels different**. Distilling your book to two or three concise questions—especially questions that pay careful attention to actors and actions—forces you to identify its central ideas. In drafting these questions, many authors realize that answering them will be a manageable task. Similarly, this chapter's exercises sometimes spark a mini "aha" moment: authors realize that their book does something slightly different from what they've said in previous meta-writing documents like job applications, fellowship applications, and book proposals.
- **You have a better understanding of the relationship between the chapters and the book as a whole**. In this chapter—as in the previous one—you'll do some preliminary work to check whether your new book questions are explicitly answered in each chapter. Doing so will continue to give you a concrete understanding of the relationship between the book and the chapters.

### Common Stumbling Blocks

- **Difficulty settling on only three book questions total**. This is a very common feeling. As we've said elsewhere, your book will do many more things than can be captured in your book questions. If you don't prioritize the most important, though, your reader will walk away from the book without a clear idea of its purpose.

- **Drafting overly complex questions**. Since this exercise allows you to add only two questions to capture what your book as a whole does, you might be tempted to try to cram every idea you want to explore into incredibly complex questions. Resist the temptation! Clarity and concision are key. Book questions are meant to help you determine your book's priorities, not to comprehensively describe your book.
- **Drafting questions that apply only to one (or a few) chapters**. In this chapter, as in the previous one, you'll evaluate several candidate book questions and check them against your chapters by producing chapter template answers. Please do this work thoroughly and make sure each book question can be answered throughout the book as a whole, not just in one or two chapters.

## EXERCISES

### Step 1: Selecting Other Book Questions

In this step, you'll brainstorm a variety of new book questions before evaluating the candidates and settling on the strongest choices.

In chapter 3, we allowed you to keep and evaluate several possible book questions. For efficiency's sake, revisit the questions you discarded and ask yourself whether any are good enough to keep. If so, copy them into the table below.

| | |
|---|---|
| Discarded alternative book question from chapter 3, step 3: | |
| Discarded alternative book question from chapter 3, step 3: | |

### Step 2: Brainstorming Questions Related to Book Question 1

With Book Question 1 (from chapter 3) in hand, use the following prompts to generate a series of related questions. When you see the phrase "the thing" in the questions below, read it as a placeholder for the main concept or idea presented in Book Question 1. For instance, "the thing" might be "innovative literary styles in twentieth-century Scandinavian novels." You don't have to *answer* the questions—just use the prompts as a springboard to generate your own questions. Ignore the prompts that don't seem relevant.

- Who does the thing?
- How does the thing occur?
- What are the effects of the thing?
- What causes the thing?
- What are important factors in the thing?
- What are the related processes?
- What are the sub-processes?

- What happens because of the thing?
- What else do we need to know to understand the thing?

| Additional book questions: | |
|---|---|
| | |

A note of caution: You may be tempted to write questions about why your project matters. But this isn't the time for that. We'll address significance in chapter 12. For now, focus on asking simple, straightforward questions about your main objects of study that you can envision answering with variations in each chapter. If your projected answer to a candidate question is the same for each chapter, it's probably a significance question—set it aside for later.

If you want inspiration, read through the following sample sets of book questions.

## RELIGIOUS STUDIES

| Book Question 1: | How did the Christian homeschooling movement of the 1990s and 2000s encourage white American homeschooling evangelicals to identify with conservative political causes? |
|---|---|
| Book Question 2: | What strategies did organizations and networks associated with the homeschooling movement use to push white American homeschooling evangelicals to transform this identification into political action? |

## CULTURAL STUDIES

| Book Question 1: | How do postcolonial ways of looking (what I call institutionalized spectacularism) define how race; racial and ethnic minority authors and artists; their works; and national identity are "packaged" and consumed in twentieth- and twenty-first-century France? |
|---|---|
| Book Question 2: | How do minority authors and artists position their works (and themselves) within a culture of institutionalized spectacularism (falling victim to them, becoming complicit within them, actively subverting them)? |

## HISTORY

| Book Question 1: | How were public dance performances intertwined with questions of citizenship and national belonging in Ireland in the early twentieth century? |
|---|---|

| Book Question 2: | How have traditional Irish folk dances helped to codify and institutionalize notions of Irishness as a cohesive national identity? |
| --- | --- |
| Book Question 3: | At the same time, how have these dances created spaces for regional embodiments of national subjectivity? |

## HISTORY

| Book Question 1: | How did a range of actors in the United States in the twentieth century explain and respond to tuberculosis outbreaks at varying scales? |
| --- | --- |
| Book Question 2: | How were individuals affected by tuberculosis outbreaks treated by medical and public health institutions? |
| Book Question 3: | How did these individuals respond to this treatment? |

## ART HISTORY

| Book Question 1: | How did hand-drawn graphic representations of Japanese origami that circulated in the first published origami instruction manuals (1797–1869) participate in a culture of what I term a "folding logic of knowledge"? |
| --- | --- |
| Book Question 2: | What are the four main ways this folding logic manifests in the larger Japanese culture of the time—both inside and beyond the practice of origami and its representation in graphics? |

## MEDIA STUDIES

| Book Question 1: | How is visual misinformation disseminated and exploited in various domains of society? |
| --- | --- |
| Book Question 2: | What threats does visual misinformation pose to US citizens? |
| Book Question 3: | How can these threats be effectively countered? |

## Step 3: Stress-Testing and Answering Your Book Questions

You should now have a list of several questions. Choose the top three or four candidates and subject them to the exercises in chapter 3 (steps 2–4). To save time, instead of doing chapter 3, step 3, as written, you can simply ask yourself: Is this the right question word for my book's main work?

For your convenience, we've summarized the chapter 3 exercises below with the tables. Complete the tables for your candidate questions.

| First Candidate Question: | |
| --- | --- |
| **Actor** in my organizing principle's question: | |

| | |
|---|---|
| Notes on actor—is this *actually* what I study in my book? Do I have the evidence to support an extended analysis of this actor? Are any important actors missing? | |
| **Action** in my organizing principle's question: | |
| Notes on action—is this *actually* what I study in my book? | |
| **Direct object** or **effect(s)** in my organizing principle's question: | |
| Notes on object or effects—is this *actually* what I show in my book? | |
| Revised question (if necessary): | |

| | |
|---|---|
| Second Candidate Question: | |
| **Actor** in my organizing principle's question: | |
| Notes on actor—is this *actually* what I study in my book? Do I have the evidence to support an extended analysis of this actor? Are any important actors missing? | |

| **Action** in my organizing principle's question: | |
| --- | --- |
| Notes on action—is this *actually* what I study in my book? | |
| **Direct object** or **effect(s)** in my organizing principle's question: | |
| Notes on object or effects—is this *actually* what I show in my book? | |
| Revised question (if necessary): | |

| Third Candidate Question: | |
| --- | --- |
| **Actor** in my organizing principle's question: | |
| Notes on actor—is this *actually* what I study in my book? Do I have the evidence to support an extended analysis of this actor? Are any important actors missing? | |
| **Action** in my organizing principle's question: | |

| Notes on action—is this *actually* what I study in my book? | |
|---|---|
| **Direct object** or **effect(s)** in my organizing principle's question: | |
| Notes on object or effects—is this *actually* what I show in my book? | |
| Revised question (if necessary): | |

| Fourth Candidate Question (optional): | |
|---|---|
| **Actor** in my organizing principle's question: | |
| Notes on actor—is this *actually* what I study in my book? Do I have the evidence to support an extended analysis of this actor? Are any important actors missing? | |
| **Action** in my organizing principle's question: | |
| Notes on action—is this *actually* what I study in my book? | |

| | |
|---|---|
| **Direct object** or **effect(s)** in my organizing principle's question: | |
| Notes on object or effects—is this *actually* what I show in my book? | |
| Revised question (if necessary): | |

Scrutinize the question words you used in the new questions: Are they right for the questions your book is asking? Revise if necessary.

In the table that follows, write down your candidate questions. Then imagine that the *only thing each chapter could do was directly answer the first question.* What would the chapter-specific answers sound like? Write a template for the answers. Don't answer the question at this point—just write a template with brackets for the chapter-specific parts.

Repeat the process for the other candidate questions.

| | |
|---|---|
| First Candidate Question: | |
| Answer Template (each chapter responds directly): | |

| | |
|---|---|
| Second Candidate Question: | |
| Answer Template (each chapter responds directly): | |

| Third Candidate Question: | |
|---|---|
| Answer Template (each chapter responds directly): | |

| Fourth Candidate Question (optional): | |
|---|---|
| Answer Template (each chapter responds directly): | |

To make sure your templates will work, think about how you would replace the brackets with phrases specific to each of your book's body chapters. Don't spend much time on this, and don't write the answers down unless you want to; just mentally test your templates to get a sense for whether they can answer the book question.

At the end, narrow down your candidate questions to *no more than two* new book questions. Most authors end up with three book questions in all, but it's fine to have just two.

## DEBRIEF, SUPPORT, AND TROUBLESHOOTING

☐ "This is it?!" or "This is it."

The punctuation communicates two very different reactions authors typically have when they reach this point. Some are surprised (or even anxious): "But this is too simple for an academic monograph!" they think. "These questions seem obvious!" This is a totally normal reaction that may stem from unreasonable expectations about what academic monographs must do. The other punctuation is meant to capture the relief other authors feel when they realize that they can indeed answer the questions—they have (or will soon have) enough material to assemble an argument.

☐ **What about the intellectual threads I want to trace that don't fit into my book questions?**

We'll say it again: your book will do many more interesting and nuanced things than can be captured in your book questions. Specifically, your book will take up several threads—important discussions that weave throughout your book, but that don't rise to the level of main claims. You will capture these threads in chapter 11.

☐ **My terminology isn't quite right.**

You might sense that your book questions' terms are not quite right—that they could benefit from minor tweaks. In chapters 5 and 10, you'll revise your work, so for now, it's best to capture these reservations and move on. If, though, you believe your terminology might be fundamentally flawed (that is, it would benefit from systematic rethinking, rather than tweaking), see appendix D.

☐ **I want to proceed with more than three book questions total.**

Force yourself to choose three for now. Later, you can swap one out for a discarded one if you need to.

| | |
|---|---|
| How did this chapter's exercises give you new insights into your project? | |
| What questions or concerns not found in the list above do you now have about your book? | |
| What might you need to think more about as you go along? Which, if any, choices would you like to revisit later? | |

## CHAPTER 5

# Revising Your Book Questions

## WHAT TO EXPECT

Typically, a writer or editor revises first with the big issues in mind (argumentation, structure, evidence use, etc.) and addresses smaller issues (style, grammar, punctuation) at a much later stage. But sometimes, pausing to consider your language before you move on can be clarifying. In this chapter's exercises, you'll make a series of passes over your book questions to ensure they ask just what you mean to ask.

### Time Investment

Expect to spend **3–4 hours** on this chapter's exercises. **Do not spend more than 5 hours** on them.

### Common Discoveries in Chapter 5

- **Your word choices affect the ideas you're communicating.** These exercises will invite you to scrutinize your language and clarify the relationships between your book's main ideas.
- **Some of your terminology is vague.** As we mentioned, when you distill your project, you'll likely find that some key terms are actually convenient placeholders for concepts you have yet to define. You can use the activities in appendixes B and D to probe them as necessary.
- **Not all of the relationships between your terms are clear.** Similarly, many authors arrive at this point knowing their book's key terms and *thinking* that the relationships between them are clear (they will, after all, have 80–100K words to elaborate, right?). When pressed, however, they discover that the promise of having thousands of words to describe these relationships was a curse: they were never forced to articulate them clearly and concisely.
- **You already know what you're saying.** Not everyone will find these exercises challenging. Authors in the social sciences, in particular, might be working with terms whose meanings are already well established and clear. If this is the case for you, do the exercises quickly and move on.

### Common Stumbling Blocks

- **Wanting to turn away from "hard questions."** Some authors realize at this point that the vocabulary they have been using might not actually describe the situations under consideration. For instance, until now, you might have said you were studying "Afrodiasporic" writers, but in this chapter you come up against a thorny question:

Can you actually consider Gabonese writers living in Côte d'Ivoire "Afrodiasporic" in the same way that Cameroonian writers living in France are? This realization can be terrifying—what if raising hard questions about your terms invalidates your whole project? But ignoring the questions won't make them go away. They may well come back at the peer review stage, when it will be much more time-consuming to fix the problems. Asking these hard questions *now* will allow you to undertake the challenging conceptual work that will ultimately lead to a more intentional and confident-sounding book.

- **Aiming for perfection**. Move quickly and respect the time limit. Remember: you *could* easily spend a lot more time to produce what you think are "perfect" book questions. But because this curriculum is iterative (you will revisit your book questions in chapter 10), the returns on your hourly investment once your book questions are "good enough" (80 percent) are infinitesimal. Revise as thoroughly as you can in the hours allotted, address the biggest concerns first, and then move on.

## EXERCISES

### Step 1: Checking Actors and Actions

Because your book questions are going to help you thread your main ideas through the chapters, it's important to make sure the actors and actions in your questions are really the ones you want to focus on. You already looked at your actors and actions in chapters 3 and 4, but here you'll examine them once more in case anything in your thinking has shifted. If you find you don't need to change much, or anything, that's fine—just go through the step quickly and move on to step 2.

First, copy your book questions below. Leave some white space below each line of writing so you can annotate the questions as necessary. If you prefer, you can type out the questions, double- or triple-space them, and print them out.

| | |
|---|---|
| Book Question 1: | |
| Book Question 2: | |
| Book Question 3 (optional): | |

Underline the actors in your questions. Draw a box around the verbs. Then ask the following questions and make notes to yourself.

1. Are the actors in these questions really the ones I'm interested in?
2. Do the verbs in my questions express what these actors will be doing across my chapters?
3. Are the questions answerable with the evidence I have?
4. Do any relationships within or between the questions need to be clarified?

It's all right if you aren't totally satisfied with your answers in this step. Just make them "good enough" and move on.

## Step 2: Stress-Testing Your Terminology

Remember that one of the core practices of this workbook is asking "hard questions" to build confidence in your project. This step pushes you to do just that.

In this exercise, you'll play the role of a skeptical reader (or peer reviewer). Attempt to raise tough questions and/or poke holes in your project's main ideas. Remember, asking these challenging questions now will ultimately produce a more intentional project and more confident prose.

Recopy your book questions in the table below, incorporating any changes you made in step 1. (If you didn't make many changes, you can reuse the table in step 1.)

| Book Question 1: | |
| --- | --- |
| Book Question 2: | |
| Book Question 3 (optional): | |

Circle the key nouns, adjectives, and verbs in each book question. Then set a timer for 25 minutes. From each word, draw arrows that point to questions or editorial comments about its definition and usage.

Note: If your terms have widely agreed-upon definitions, as they often do in the social sciences, you don't need to scrutinize them as thoroughly. In this case, double-check that that term is appropriate for what you study and move on (even without using the full 25 minutes). For instance, if one of your book questions is about "voters," double-check that "voters" is the most appropriate term (and not, say, "politically engaged citizens," "people who cast ballots in [election]," or "people registered to vote in [election]") and go on to the next term. If you're studying more nebulous terms (like "neoliberalism," "power," or "visibility"), you should examine them more carefully.

**Sample Question Bank:**
- Is this really what I'm studying? Is this really what I mean to say?
- What other terms could I use instead of this one? What are their shortcomings? Advantages?
- What X am I talking about?
- How does Y occur?
- Define Z. Or, what does Z mean?
- If I use "X and Y," are both terms essential? Is there a single term that would capture my meaning?

Now set the timer for an additional 25 minutes. Look back over your comments and questions. Respond to the three or four issues you deem most important; then revise your book questions as necessary.

## Step 3: Assessing Conceptual Relationships

In this step, you'll identify the key terms in your book questions and reflect on their relationships. The purpose of this exercise is to think about how your book questions are connected. Eventually, in chapter 12, you'll transform your book questions into your book argument. It's important, then, to aim for questions that build on each other, rather than simply questions about the same topic.

Look back at your book questions and circle all of the "keywords"—essential words or phrases, especially those that are specific enough that someone might use them to search for your book.

Now look at your keywords together. How is each one related to the others? Freewrite and/or draw a diagram to define the relationships among the keywords.

| Relationships among keywords: | |
| --- | --- |
| | |

Now examine your book questions in the table in step 2 in light of what you've just learned. In the box below, freewrite and/or draw a diagram to express the relationships among the questions. If necessary, update the questions to reflect your most current understanding of them.

Note: If the relationships among your terms and questions seem so straightforward that you're wondering what the point of this exercise is, that's fine! Some authors' terms are more complicated to deal with than yours are. Just sketch out your relationships briefly and move on to the next step.

Relationships among
book questions:

## Step 4: Projecting Your Chapter Answers

As a final step, we'd like you to revisit the chapter answer templates that you developed in chapters 3 and 4. Recall that these templates were a way of quickly checking whether your book questions could generate workable and distinct answers for every chapter. We want to bring them up again to do a deeper dive into the structure of your book questions.

One difficulty that authors sometimes run into is that all of their chapter answers to a given book question sound repetitive. Consider the following book question and the corresponding chapter answer template. This hypothetical book is about visual misinformation, and each chapter addresses visual misinformation in a different social domain.

**In which domains of society is visual misinformation disseminated?**

Chapter 1: In [domain of society], visual misinformation is disseminated.
Chapter 2: In [domain of society], visual misinformation is disseminated.
Chapter 3: In [domain of society], visual misinformation is disseminated.

You can immediately see that these chapter answers are going to end up sounding fairly boring. On the surface, they seem to check all the boxes—the question is clear, the answers are differentiated, the template is based on the question. But it isn't clear whether we're learning anything new in each chapter about the concept of visual misinformation. Ideally, we would expect this book to illustrate a different facet or aspect of visual misinformation in each chapter, so that we arrived at the end with a comprehensive understanding of the nuances of this concept. Instead, what we get is: "In educational settings, visual misinformation is disseminated. On social media, visual misinformation is also disseminated. In healthcare, visual misinformation is *also* disseminated." This isn't a compelling narrative! The reader may wonder why they have to read a whole book to grasp it. What can we learn about visual misinformation from the second, third, and fourth chapters that we can't learn from the first?

We would advise this author to think about what new aspect or form of visual misinformation we will learn about in each chapter. Each chapter might explain something about visual misinformation that we can only understand by examining how it operates in a particular social domain. Together, the chapters will paint a complete picture of the central concept.

If you find yourself in a similar position, we have a specific piece of advice for you: embrace the word "how." Observe how the question and answers change when the visual misinformation author rewrites her question as a "how" question:

**How is visual misinformation disseminated in various domains of society?**

**Chapter 1**: In [domain], [visual misinformation is disseminated in one way].
**Chapter 2**: In [domain], [it's disseminated in another way].
**Chapter 3**: In [domain], [it's disseminated in yet another way].

In chapter 2, for instance, we may learn about how deepfakes and misleading graphs acquire credibility when they are shared in social networks. In chapter 3, we may learn about how the trappings of celebrity interact with trust in medical authority to increase the appeal of health-related infographics. (The author may want to think about whether each chapter is going to focus on a particular type of visual misinformation.) Notice that each chapter answer is written so that the most predictable aspect of the sentence comes first, and the most interesting and distinctive aspect of the sentence comes *last*—this is a clever rhetorical choice that emphasizes the book's intellectual richness.

Recopy your revised book questions in the table below (or type them up and print them out). Below each question, write your chapter answer template from chapter 3, step 4. Then, using the template, write out a very rough answer to the question for each of your chapters (excluding any background/historical/conceptual chapters, the introduction, and the conclusion). If you wrote down your chapter answers in chapter 3, step 4, you can copy them here. Spend as little time on your chapter answers as possible—this exercise is just meant to help you check your book questions. You'll give the chapter answers the attention they deserve in chapter 9.

| Book Question 1: | |
|---|---|
| Answer Template: | |

| Chapter Answers: | |
|---|---|

| Book Question 2: | |
|---|---|
| Answer Template: | |
| Chapter Answers: | |

| Book Question 3 (optional): | |
|---|---|

| Answer Template: | |
|---|---|
| Chapter Answers: | |

With the visual misinformation book example in mind, examine your book question and chapter answers. Are your chapter answers repetitive? Can you tweak the book question and/or the answer template so that each chapter answer adds a new facet to your book narrative? Make any revisions that occur to you.

If you still feel hesitant about your book questions, you can consult the more robust tools in appendixes B and D. But you'll review your questions in chapter 9–10, so they don't need to be in their final form at this point.

## DEBRIEF, SUPPORT, AND TROUBLESHOOTING

☐ **I still feel like I can't get my book questions right**.

This feeling is *very, very* common. You will return to and revise your book questions when you reach chapters 9–10. If, at this point, you have *serious* reservations about the terminology you use to articulate your book's key concepts, consult appendix D.

☐ **I worry that my book questions are still too simple for a book "main idea" or "argument."**

This feeling, too, is very common. But many books' questions and arguments are surprisingly simple. It's in the chapters, when you analyze your evidence and show the various ways the central questions can be answered, that your book will reveal the full picture of its originality and nuance.

Remember, too, that the book questions may only seem simple to you because you're so familiar with them. To someone else, they will likely seem fresh and intriguing.

☐ **This exercise has shown me that a chapter is being pulled in two directions—one focused on people and another on abstract practices, processes, or events. How can I center both?**

While completing the chapter 5 work, some authors—especially those studying both events or practices and people—discover a tension in the way they're telling their story. Specifically, they realize that their chapters will likely need to focus on *either* the people (subordinating the practices and events) *or* the practices and events (subordinating the people). There is no one right answer—they're just different stories. If you plan to center the events (or practices), you might consider keeping the people-centered stories as anecdotes for your chapters' introductions. Or you could consider nontraditional chapter structures (like having a person-centered "interlude" following each chapter). In any case, please consult your model books and ask colleagues and mentors about your options.

| | |
|---|---|
| How did this chapter's exercises give you new insights into your project? | |
| What questions or concerns not found in the list above do you now have about your book? | |
| What might you need to think more about as you go along? Which, if any, choices would you like to revisit later? | |

## CHAPTER 6

# Assessing Your Chapters on Their Own Terms

## WHAT TO EXPECT

In this chapter, you will lay out your book's chapters as you understand them currently. Work with all body chapters, including those you plan to write but have not yet written.

### Time Investment

Expect to spend **about 4 hours** on these exercises. **Do not spend more than 6 hours** on them.

### Common Discoveries in Chapter 6

- **You gain increased clarity about what your book is—and, equally importantly, what it is not.** Evaluating specific dimensions of your chapters will give you new insight into their broadest scale.
- **You can more easily identify your book's extraneous parts.** Completing these exercises immediately after drafting and revising your book questions can help you identify what will be critical in each chapter, given your new understanding of the book's priorities.
- **You had never asked fundamental questions about your evidence base or chapters.** I (Katelyn) did not have this realization until the high-stakes milestone of peer review, when my reviewers rightly asked me pointed questions about my book's evidence base and chapters' composition. They asked, for instance: Why do you analyze *this* novel (and *only* this novel) in this chapter? Why does less well-known author A deserve to be considered alongside famous authors B and C? In this chapter's exercises, we ask you similarly pointed questions so that you can consider these dimensions of your book well before the peer review stage.
- **You are in charge of your book, and there is no one "right" path.** In chapter 2, the work you did to evaluate organizing principles likely helped you realize that you're in the "driver's seat." Similarly, in this chapter, you'll get to decide which of dozens of chapter configurations would best support your book's main claims.

### Common Stumbling Blocks

- **A growing sense that a chapter does not belong.** If you make this discovery: celebrate it! While eliminating chapters can be frustrating or painful, take comfort in two things. First, doing so is the quickest way to produce a more coherent, effective book. Second, this book is not your only opportunity to write about these topics, works, or case studies. If it seems helpful, sketch out a quick plan for publishing the material you cut.

- **An urge to stop and do research.** When completing the exercises for chapters that don't yet exist, work quickly, based on what you know now. Now is not the time to stop your higher-order work to do additional research or reading.
- **Challenges answering questions about chapters you haven't written yet.** This is to be expected. If you haven't written a chapter yet, complete the exercises as best you can, given the information you have now. The good news is that completing these exercises before you've written the chapter can help you research and write the chapter more quickly.

## EXERCISES

### Step 1: Producing Chapter Snapshots

In chapters 3–5, you clarified your book's core priorities via your book questions. Soon (in chapter 9) you'll answer those questions for each chapter. But first we're going to spend some time considering each chapter as a complete unit and reviewing its role within your book.

First, take a moment to review your book questions and the table you filled out in chapter 1, step 1.

Then use the following prompts to describe each of your book's chapters. For chapters you haven't yet written or claims you haven't developed, just make your best guess.

Here's how this exercise would look for a book illustrating how four contemporary Indigenous sculptors produce their own styles of sculpture and "indigenize" sculpture itself in different ways.

**ART HISTORY**

| 1: Chapter #: | 1 | 2: Chapter topic: | [Sculptor A's] use of Indigenous tools to produce 2 well-known pieces |
|---|---|---|---|
| 3: Chapter scope and evidence type: | One artist (one site, narrow chronological scope) and two main pieces | | |
| 4: Chapter main claim(s): | [Sculptor A] indigenizes sculpture by using Indigenous tools on classical materials to represent Indigenous subjects. | | |

| 1: Chapter #: | 2 | 2: Chapter topic: | Indigenized practices and their reception in [sculptor B's] corpus |
|---|---|---|---|
| 3: Chapter scope and evidence type: | One artist but their entire thirty-year corpus. Critical reception (reviews, scholarship) plus vast array of works (well-known, lesser-known, public, private, various materials, etc.) | | |
| 4: Chapter main claim(s): | [Sculptor B] indigenizes sculpture through an evolving range of strategies, to varied racially, ethnically, and nationally inflected acclaim or critique. | | |

| 1: Chapter #: | 3 | 2: Chapter topic: | Indigenized practices of [sculptor C] and the traditions on which they draw |
|---|---|---|---|

| 3: Chapter scope and evidence type: | Fairly narrow scope: two series by one artist exhibited in one year, plus participant interviews, family genealogies, oral histories, classical curricula, and exhibition speeches |
|---|---|
| 4: Chapter main claim(s): | [Sculptor C] indigenizes the creative process by drawing from and employing embodied cultural practices not typically found in classical training curricula. |

| 1: Chapter #: | 4 | 2: Chapter topic: | Indigenized sculptures and their meta-commentary (signage) by [sculptor D] plus audience reactions to them |
|---|---|---|---|
| 3: Chapter scope and evidence type: | Fairly narrow: three publicly commissioned large-scale sculptures in 3 US sites plus hidden-camera footage of viewer reactions, 2019 ||||
| 4: Chapter main claim(s): | [Sculptor D] develops the practice of "indigenized overwriting" through works and their metacommentary, which explicitly educates the public about how to decolonize the gaze. ||||

And here are the tables for a book about how amateur and professional musicians navigate a dominant club practice—requiring bands to "pay-to-play" (rather than receiving compensation to play), often by buying a predetermined number of tickets to their own show that they are expected to resell.

## SOCIOLOGY/ETHNOMUSICOLOGY

| 1: Chapter #: | 1 | 2: Chapter topic: | The emergence and dominance of the pay-to-play model in popular US music |
|---|---|---|---|
| 3: Chapter scope and evidence type: | Broad, multi-sited and longitudinal (1920–2005) scope, using historical sources and interviews (with musicians and club owners) ||||
| 4: Chapter main claim(s): | The particular interwar economic climate led popular music club owners to experiment with several economic models; one of these, the general pay-to-play model, came to dominate major metropolises. By the 1980s, the model had shifted into a less obvious—but no less difficult for musicians—form: requiring artists to buy and resell their own tickets. ||||

| 1: Chapter #: | 2 | 2: Chapter topic: | The range of responses 26 jazz musicians in 5 sites develop to the pay-to-play model, 2007–2009 |
|---|---|---|---|
| 3: Chapter scope and evidence type: | Broad, multi-sited geographical scope but narrow chronological scope; broad range of individuals represented; evidence is participant observation and personal interviews ||||
| 4: Chapter main claim(s): | The individual jazz artists under consideration develop a range of stances (each with varying outcomes) toward the pay-to-play model; of these, some factors seem to have a weak correlation with more favorable economic outcomes. ||||

| 1: Chapter #: | 3 | 2: Chapter topic: | The strategies several amateur rock groups with no professional aspirations use to navigate the Whiskey a Go Go's pre-paid ticket policy |
|---|---|---|---|

| 3: Chapter scope and evidence type: | Narrow focus on three groups and one venue, 2008–2013, using participant observation and recorded interviews |
|---|---|
| 4: Chapter main claim(s): | These groups adopt two main strategies to lessen the economic impact of this policy, but, in the absence of large groups of fans that would come with professional musical aspirations, these artists face a particular challenge: they must choose between self-subsidizing stage time (with no hope of recouping their payment) or relying on networks of strong ties (friends, family members, and close social circles) to bear this economic burden for them. |

| 1: Chapter #: | 4 | 2: Chapter topic: | The strategies 12 hopeful professional pop/country artists in Nashville use to navigate various venues' pay-to-play policies |
|---|---|---|---|
| 3: Chapter scope and evidence type: | Narrow focus on several individuals and several venues in one location, 2008–2013, using participant observation and recorded interviews ||| 
| 4: Chapter main claim(s): | This group is able to spread the economic burden to a much larger extended network of weak ties—budding fans—than the amateurs can, and therefore they have a higher chance of recouping their ticket costs. However, this ability to recoup pay-to-play costs (and earn a small profit) often requires a different economic or opportunity cost that can cancel out their profits: hiring social media managers or choosing to manage marketing themselves, which requires investing hundreds of unpaid hours. |||

| 1: Chapter #: | 5 | 2: Chapter topic: | Several case studies of one particular role opened up by this model—the social media influencer—plus analysis of content that helps artists the most (and their economic models) |
|---|---|---|---|
| 3: Chapter scope and evidence type: | Four specific top social media influencers' posts, plus marketing materials and interviews ||| 
| 4: Chapter main claim(s): | In the era of pay-to-play and social media, a new niche job/role has opened up—the social media influencer—that has a key role in helping artists navigate this model. Several specific types of content tend to help artists, depending on their genre and professional aspirations. |||

| 1: Chapter #: | 6 | 2: Chapter topic: | The pay-to-play model during the COVID-19 shutdown of live music venues and the "pivot" to online platforms like Spotify and YouTube |
|---|---|---|---|
| 3: Chapter scope and evidence type: | Narrow, event-focused scope, but broad geographical and genre scope. Looks at Spotify, YouTube, and livestream platform guidelines, interviews, industry news sources, and participant observation. ||| 
| 4: Chapter main claim(s): | Surprisingly, vestiges of the pay-to-play model persist in seemingly more democratic digital platforms after physical venues shut down. |||

**YOUR CHAPTER SNAPSHOTS**

| 1: Chapter #: | | 2: Chapter topic: | |
|---|---|---|---|
| **3: Chapter scope and evidence type:** | | | |
| **4: Chapter main claim(s):** | | | |

| 1: Chapter #: | | 2: Chapter topic: | |
|---|---|---|---|
| **3: Chapter scope and evidence type:** | | | |
| **4: Chapter main claim(s):** | | | |

| 1: Chapter #: | | 2: Chapter topic: | |
|---|---|---|---|
| 3: Chapter scope and evidence type: | | | |
| 4: Chapter main claim(s): | | | |

| 1: Chapter #: | | 2: Chapter topic: | |
|---|---|---|---|
| 3: Chapter scope and evidence type: | | | |
| 4: Chapter main claim(s): | | | |

| 1: Chapter #: | | 2: Chapter topic: | |
|---|---|---|---|
| 3: Chapter scope and evidence type: | | | |
| 4: Chapter main claim(s): | | | |

| 1: Chapter #: | | 2: Chapter topic: | |
|---|---|---|---|
| 3: Chapter scope and evidence type: | | | |
| 4: Chapter main claim(s): | | | |

*Want Additional Practice?* --------------------------------------------------------------

Complete a table for two chapters from your model book(s).

## Step 2: Surveying Your Chapters within Your Book

Reflecting on the answers you just wrote, assess whether the chapters add up to the book and whether each one individually advances your book's claims.

A quick reminder: we are intentionally asking you pointed clarifying questions that you might prefer to avoid answering. It's *totally normal* for these questions to make authors uncomfortable, and it's fine if you're not 100 percent sure about your answers—nothing is set in stone at this point. That said, it's important for you to take these types of questions seriously, for two reasons. First, if you don't deal proactively with any problems, peer reviewers will likely ask you similar questions. Second, producing and revising chapters takes a lot of time. We don't want you to sink dozens (if not hundreds) of hours into perfecting a chapter only to realize much later that it does not actually fit your book.

| | |
|---|---|
| Taken together, will my chapters allow me to fully answer my book questions? If not, what could I add? | |
| Do two or more chapters overlap significantly in scope or topic? Can I eliminate one or combine them? | |
| Does any chapter seem significantly different in size, scope, or approach from the others? If so, what could I do? | |

## Step 3: Assessing the Alignment between Your Chapters' Evidence, Scope, and Claims

As you learned in chapter 1 of this workbook, your book's claims as a whole depend on the evidence you will mobilize to support them. You're also beginning to see that each chapter will play an important role in helping you develop your book's argument. In step 2 of this chapter, you already assessed whether each chapter contributes to your book's overall claim.

But for the chapter to be able to advance your book-level argument, each chapter must make a standalone claim that is commensurate with the evidence it presents. In this step, you'll ensure that each chapter's main claim is truly aligned with the evidence it presents.

First, review the material on the alignment between scope, claims, and evidence found in chapter 1, step 2, of this workbook and our suggestions on how to troubleshoot misaligned claims, scope, and evidence in chapter 1, step 3.

Next, for each of your book's body chapters (in turn), consider the answers in boxes 3 and 4 of the tables you filled out in step 1 of this chapter. With the information about the alignment between claims, scope, and evidence fresh in your mind, complete the following table:

| Chapter #: | | Are the claims, scope, and evidence well aligned? (Yes/No) | |
|---|---|---|---|
| If "no," this is how I think I can ensure they align better: | | | |
| What other thoughts come to mind about the alignment between my chapter's scope, claims, and evidence? | | | |

| Chapter #: | | Are the claims, scope, and evidence well aligned? (Yes/No) | |
|---|---|---|---|
| If "no," this is how I think I can ensure they align better: | | | |

| What other thoughts come to mind about the alignment between my chapter's scope, claims, and evidence? | |
|---|---|
| | |

| Chapter #: | | Are the claims, scope, and evidence well aligned? (Yes/No) | |
|---|---|---|---|
| If "no," this is how I think I can ensure they align better: | | | |
| What other thoughts come to mind about the alignment between my chapter's scope, claims, and evidence? | | | |

| Chapter #: | | Are the claims, scope, and evidence well aligned? (Yes/No) | |
|---|---|---|---|
| If "no," this is how I think I can ensure they align better: | | | |
| What other thoughts come to mind about the alignment between my chapter's scope, claims, and evidence? | | | |

| Chapter #: | | Are the claims, scope, and evidence well aligned? (Yes/No) | |
|---|---|---|---|
| If "no," this is how I think I can ensure they align better: | | | |

| What other thoughts come to mind about the alignment between my chapter's scope, claims, and evidence? | |
|---|---|
| | |

| Chapter #: | | Are the claims, scope, and evidence well aligned? (Yes/No) | |
|---|---|---|---|
| If "no," this is how I think I can ensure they align better: | | | |
| What other thoughts come to mind about the alignment between my chapter's scope, claims, and evidence? | | | |

## Step 4: Evaluating Your Chapters' Corpus

Another question peer reviewers will ask about your project as a whole—and about each individual chapter—is whether the evidence you have chosen truly constitutes a representative sample of the types of claims you are making. That is, they will ask whether you have cherry-picked evidence that fits your claims and ignored other evidence that doesn't fit, and whether you have chosen the *best* examples among all of the possible evidence.

The best way we've found to push authors to see this dimension of their chapters through reviewers' eyes is to ask a pointed question: "Why did you choose this collection of sources, and not any other pieces of evidence you *could* have chosen?" This question presumes that there is a larger corpus of evidence you have sifted through and that you have deliberately made choices on this front.

For instance, when I (Katelyn) got to the peer review stage, a reviewer noted that many of the texts and authors I study in my book are well known; in this regard, my second chapter on a less well-studied text seemed an outlier. A reviewer asked: "Why only *one* novel? And why only *this* novel?"

These questions helped me realize that I had reasons for these choices. But because they seemed obvious to me, I hadn't articulated them in my book. Now we're asking you to record your own reasons.

For each of your book's body chapters, complete the following table:

| Chapter #: | | Other pieces of evidence I *could* mobilize but don't: | |
|---|---|---|---|
| Why this corpus (and not other pieces of evidence)? | | | |
| Reflect on this task: Is my evidence representative? How could I deal with any problems? | | | |

| Chapter #: | | Other pieces of evidence I *could* mobilize but don't: | |
|---|---|---|---|
| Why this corpus (and not other pieces of evidence)? | | | |
| Reflect on this task: Is my evidence representative? How could I deal with any problems? | | | |

| Chapter #: | | Other pieces of evidence I *could* mobilize but don't: | |
|---|---|---|---|
| Why this corpus (and not other pieces of evidence)? | | | |

| Reflect on this task: Is my evidence representative? How could I deal with any problems? | |
|---|---|

| Chapter #: | | Other pieces of evidence I *could* mobilize but don't: | |
|---|---|---|---|
| Why this corpus (and not other pieces of evidence)? | | | |
| Reflect on this task: Is my evidence representative? How could I deal with any problems? | | | |

| Chapter #: | | Other pieces of evidence I *could* mobilize but don't: | |
|---|---|---|---|
| Why this corpus (and not other pieces of evidence)? | | | |
| Reflect on this task: Is my evidence representative? How could I deal with any problems? | | | |

| Chapter #: | | Other pieces of evidence I *could* mobilize but don't: | |
|---|---|---|---|
| Why this corpus (and not other pieces of evidence)? | | | |
| Reflect on this task: Is my evidence representative? How could I deal with any problems? | | | |

## Step 5: Adding Metacommentary

Most academic authors are used to talking about what their work "says," "shows," or "argues." But each unit of your writing (book, chapter, paragraph, sentence) also performs a task—it might give background, offer and analyze direct evidence, discuss implications, or generalize one example to a larger pattern.

You know that your chapters are all *saying* (or claiming) different things, but you might be only vaguely aware of what they're *doing* to serve the book. You might even worry that, when you boil it all down, your book will sound like a collection of examples that all show the same thing: "A shows X, and B also shows X, and C also shows X . . ."

In this step, you'll look back at your chapter tables, ask whether it's clear what the chapter is *doing* that's new and different (beyond just considering a different example), and add some metacommentary about the chapter.

Let's review the "indigenizing sculpture" book. We could summarize each chapter like this:

**Topic**: How [sculptor] produces indigenized sculpture
**Claim**: [Chapter-specific sculptor] produces indigenized sculpture in [chapter-specific way].

This is a perfectly acceptable start to a solid book! But notice that the book seems to consist of four independent case studies that all illustrate similar things. The main idea starts to sound a little repetitive.

We suspect that this book has the potential to tell a more dynamic, interesting story—to explore a fresh angle of its topic in every chapter. We would ask this author: How does making [chapter-specific claim] give us *new insight* into the book's central concept of indigenizing sculpture? What does this chapter tell us about indigenizing sculpture that none of the other chapters does?

We'd invite this author to return to the table in step 1 and add notes to box 4 ("Chapter main claim(s)") about the new insight each chapter contributes. Here's what they might say:

**ART HISTORY**

|  | Metacommentary |
|---|---|
| Chapter 1: | This chapter illustrates how indigenizing media happens within the studio space. |
| Chapter 2: | This chapter shows the risks of indigenizing media and the impact of such a strategy on career opportunities. |
| Chapter 3: | This chapter traces how indigenizing media is not just about subject, material, and practices, but also about knowledge, lineage, and training. |
| Chapter 4: | This chapter shows that indigenizing is also a process of educating the viewer. |

The pay-to-play musician book might seem less repetitive, but let's take a look at it too. The topic and claims of chapters 2, 3, and 4 turn out to say similar things:

**Topic**: How [chapter-specific artist group] navigates the pay-to-play model in [city, genre]
**Claim**: [Chapter-specific artist group] navigates the pay-to-play model in [city, genre] in [this chapter-specific way] with [this chapter-specific effect].

This author will want to add metacommentary about these chapters by asking: How does making [chapter-specific claim] give us new insight into the pay-to-play model (and/or artists' ability to negotiate it)?

Remember, we're just jotting down notes, not drafting perfectly polished ideas. Focusing only on the chapters with the most similar claims and topics (chapters 2–4), this author might say:

**SOCIOLOGY/ETHNOMUSICOLOGY**

|  | Metacommentary |
|---|---|
| Chapter 2: | The broad case of jazz musicians allows me to establish a vast range of concrete examples of the types of responses to the pay-to-play model. |
| Chapter 3: | The specific case of the amateur rock groups with no professional aspirations illustrates that certain dimensions of the pay-to-play model have less impact on musicians who do not care about future career trajectories, but at a trade-off: they have to rely on family and friends instead of fans. |
| Chapter 4: | The specific case of individual pop and country musicians with professional aspirations shows how the artists develop unique responses to the pay-to-play model filtered through the already demanding constraints of music industry expectations. |

Now it's your turn. Fill out the table below to add metacommentary about your chapters. Refer back to the chapter snapshots in step 1 as necessary. If you find two chapters that don't seem to add anything new to the reader's understanding of your book's main topic or central concept(s), ask whether both chapters are truly necessary in your book. What would happen if you eliminated one or combined them?

|  | Metacommentary |
|---|---|
| Chapter 1: |  |
| Chapter 2: |  |
| Chapter 3: |  |

| Chapter 4: | |
|---|---|
| Chapter 5: | |
| Chapter 6: | |

## DEBRIEF, SUPPORT, AND TROUBLESHOOTING

☐ **I suspect that one (or more) chapter does not belong.**

This fairly common discovery can be good news: not only will cutting extraneous chapters make your remaining manuscript more coherent, but you can also spin this writing off into other publications. If you are not yet sure whether a chapter belongs, hold on to it for now. In the next chapter, you will learn an additional tool—a concept we call "parallelism"—to help you decide.

☐ **I'm starting to understand why experts recommend you immediately cut "lit review," "background," or "methods" chapters (but at the same time, now I'm wondering where that material belongs).**

Of course, not all disciplines are the same. Please defer to your model books or mentors in your field regarding your discipline's (and/or target publisher's) tolerance for chapters (other than the book introduction) whose sole purpose is to give background information, review the literature, outline methods, or develop a theory. That said, this chapter's exercises likely showed you that in most humanities disciplines (and some social sciences), readers expect each chapter to tangibly advance the book's narrative. Background, methods, and lit review chapters do not do so. For a more thorough discussion of such chapters, see William Germano's *From Dissertation to Book*, chapter 5.

☐ **I'm beginning to see that my book's structure and chapter contents will need work.**

Some authors realize that some of their body chapters (sometimes up to half!) existed only to offer background for the "real" case studies. Others realize that two chapters overlap significantly and do not make substantially different points. Still others begin to see that their book has two (or more) parts. In chapter 7, we'll give you additional ways to assess your chapters and their similarity to each other. For now, capture your thoughts about your book's and chapters' structure.

| How did this chapter's exercises give you new insights into your project? | |
| --- | --- |
| What questions or concerns not found in the list above do you now have about your book? | |
| What might you need to think more about as you go along? Which, if any, choices would you like to revisit later? | |

## CHAPTER 7

# Checking Your Chapters for Parallelism

## WHAT TO EXPECT

Now that you know (more or less) that your chapters serve your book and how they do so, it's time to make sure their scope and structure serve your book's overarching claims. In this step, you will consider how the current or potential structure of your chapters might affect the lessons your reader gleans from your book.

You will do this using a framework we call *parallelism*, which involves identifying constants and variables across your chapters. You already encountered parallelism on a macro scale when you identified your book's main organizing principle (and perhaps a secondary organizing principle) in chapter 2.

In the exercises in this chapter, however, you will see that your book's chapters differ from one another in many other ways. These differences will affect your reader's experience of your claims.

### Time Investment

Expect to spend **about 4** hours on the exercises in this chapter. **Do not spend more than 6 hours** on them.

### Common Discoveries in Chapter 7

- **You feel that your book is shifting even more beneath you and that certain things are not quite right.** This is normal, and working through this uncertainty is the only way to gain clarity. Things will come together soon enough.
- **Your book has more variables than you expected.** Before doing this work, you might have had a vague sense that your chapters were different from one another, but many authors are surprised to see just how many variables they identify using these exercises.

### Common Stumbling Blocks

- **Thinking your book has fewer variables than it does.** Once you start identifying variables in your own project, you will see handfuls of potential variables. Sometimes this realization can overwhelm authors, who believe these apparent inconsistencies between chapters weaken their book. Consequently, they resist listing variables they consider "inconsequential." As we underscore in what follows, your goal in this chapter is not to *resolve* all the non-parallelisms, but just to know they exist.
- **Wanting to resolve every non-parallelism you find.** Not every variable shifts the frame so much that it detracts from your reader's ability to follow your main claims. In fact,

reading a book that's exactly parallel in all dimensions (aside from its organizing principle) would likely be boring. So, while you should know what non-parallelisms your book contains, you won't need to resolve every non-parallelism you find.

- **Wondering where and how to justify these non-parallelisms.** When you see these small (or large) differences among chapters, you might fret: "How on earth am I going to justify all these non-parallelisms?" The good news: you don't need to explicitly justify all (or even the majority) of them. Rather, you likely need to justify only those that your reviewers or readers might find problematic. Typically, this work happens either in the book's introduction or in chapter introductions. Here's a rule of thumb to keep in mind: err on the side of *under*-justifying, since, when done poorly or too often, it can read as hedging or defensiveness.

## EXERCISES

### Step 1: Identifying Constants and Variables

All books have what we call "variables," or elements that change from chapter to chapter, and "constants," or elements that are held consistent across the book.

Imagine you're writing a book about the life cycle of a tree. There are thousands of ways to tell this story. Here are three:

**BOOK A**

| Chapter 1: | An elm tree, physiologically, from seed to sprout |
|---|---|
| Chapter 2: | An elm tree, physiologically, from sprout to sapling |
| Chapter 3: | An elm tree, physiologically, from sapling to its first reproduction cycle |
| Chapter 4: | An elm tree, physiologically, from its first reproduction cycle to its death |

| Constants: | type of tree, number of trees, methodology/lens (physiology) |
|---|---|
| Variables: | point of life cycle |

Note that this book's structure foregrounds lessons about the tree's life cycle. Its implied audience is someone curious to learn about the physiology of elm trees at various life stages.

**BOOK B**

| Chapter 1: | An elm tree's life cycle, seen through the eyes of a bird |
|---|---|
| Chapter 2: | An elm tree's life cycle, seen through the eyes of a squirrel |
| Chapter 3: | An elm tree's life cycle, seen through the eyes of a human |
| Chapter 4: | An elm tree's life cycle, seen through the eyes of microbes |

| Constants: | type of tree, number of trees, number of species' experience, period of life cycle (whole thing) |
|---|---|
| Variables: | type of species' experience |

This imaginary book's structure foregrounds lessons about how different species experience trees. Its implied audience is someone curious to learn how different species interact with elm trees.

**BOOK C**

| Chapter 1: | How to sprout an acorn |
|---|---|
| Chapter 2: | A worm's experience of an elm tree's sprout |
| Chapter 3: | How to use fertilizer to grow pine trees from sapling to maturity |
| Chapter 4: | Animals that thrive in oak tree forests |

| Constants: | few |
|---|---|
| Variables: | number of trees (an acorn vs. oak tree forest), purpose (how to vs. informational), perspective (worm vs. scholar), type of tree (oak, elm, pine), point of life cycle (seed, sprout, sapling, mature) |

Unlike books A and B, this collection of chapters doesn't suggest a clear book-level narrative. Similarly, it's hard to conceive of one audience that would be interested in the entire book. Someone wanting practical, "how-to" information might be interested in chapters 1 and 3, but they're about different tree types.

Of course, we fabricated these hyperbolic examples to illustrate our argument about parallelism—rarely are books as neat as examples A or B or as messy as example C. So let's examine a book about labor history in the urban South. The table below shows a condensed version of the book's chapter snapshots.

*THE URBAN SOUTH: A LABOR HISTORY*

| Chapter 1 snapshot: | Social conditions of factory laborers in the urban South, 1900–1950, told through historical sources |
|---|---|
| Chapter 2 snapshot: | The opening day of the Wonder Bread factory in Memphis, 1921, told through eyewitness testimony and newspapers |
| Chapter 3 snapshot: | Legal history of manufacturing labor contracts in Tennessee, Arkansas, and Louisiana, 1910–1943 |
| Chapter 4 snapshot: | Governmental interventions in Tennessee to protect workers' rights, post-1923, told through historical sources |
| Chapter 5 snapshot: | Ground-up labor union organization in Orleans parish, 1945–1950, told through oral history |
| Chapter 6 snapshot: | Interstate highway system's impact on labor conditions in the urban South post-1965, told through businesses' incident reports and internal memos |
| Coda snapshot: | The Wonder Bread factory closing in 2012 |

To identify the variables, ask yourself: What changes from chapter to chapter? The following table lists some ideas.

| Variables often found in humanities and social science books (check all that apply): | |
| --- | --- |
| ☐ Author, group, or event under consideration | ☐ Geographical scope (neighborhood, city, state, region, continent) |
| ☐ Type of evidence (novels, semi-structured interviews, archival sources) | ☐ Positionality of authors, interviewees, or actors (nationality, age, education, language background) |
| ☐ Number of works, case studies, events, sites, interviewees | ☐ Site or setting of work, events, case studies, interviews |
| ☐ Chronological scope (days, months, years, centuries) | ☐ Medium and/or formal characteristics (print, video, audio, realism, pointillism) |
| ☐ Audience or sector type (public, private) | ☐ Process, theme, or characteristic under consideration |

Here's what stands out to us. This author's organizing principle seems to be roughly chronological (each chapter examines a different historical "moment"), and each chapter seems to engage her book's topic (a "labor history of the urban South"). But notice how many variables quickly emerge.

- **Author, group, or event under consideration**: the laborers themselves vs. labor unions vs. businesses vs. government (at a variety of scales)
- **Chronological scope**: 50 years vs. one day vs. 30-ish years vs. 5 years vs. vague period (post-1965)
- **Type of evidence**: historical sources (2 chapters) vs. testimony and newspapers/oral history (2 chapters) vs. labor contracts vs. incident reports and memos
- **Geographical scope**: region (urban South; Tennessee, Arkansas, and Louisiana), city (Memphis), state (Tennessee), county (Orleans parish)
- **Site or setting of case studies**: Tennessee is represented in six chapters, while two are about Louisiana
- **Sector type**: governmental interventions (public) vs. labor contracts (private)
- **Theme under consideration**: highways vs. social conditions vs. labor unions vs. a factory vs. legal history, etc.

And those are just the variables we can identify based on the chapter snapshots! We can also easily imagine that the book might have other variables—like the positionality of the interviewees.

Now it's your turn to identify variables in your own book. The checklist below lists variables that often appear in books in the humanities and qualitative social sciences. Check off any that appear in your book. Then add anything else that changes from chapter to chapter.

| Variables often found in humanities and social science books (check all that apply): | |
| --- | --- |
| ☐ Author, group, or event under consideration | ☐ Geographical scope (neighborhood, city, state, region, continent) |
| ☐ Type of evidence (novels, semi-structured interviews, archival sources) | ☐ Positionality of authors, interviewees, or actors (nationality, age, education, language background) |

| ☐ Number of works, case studies, events, sites, interviewees | ☐ Site or setting of work, events, case studies, interviews |
|---|---|
| ☐ Chronological scope (days, months, years, centuries) | ☐ Medium and/or formal characteristics (print, video, audio, realism, pointillism) |
| ☐ Audience or sector type (public, private) | ☐ Process, theme, or characteristic under consideration |
| **Other variables in this book (list):** | |
| | |

Before proceeding, take a quick glance back at the chapter answer templates you produced in chapter 5, step 4. Do you see any variables you haven't listed? If so, add them.

## Step 2: Evaluating Your Book's Variables

Let's think about what kind of story these variables tell. When something changes from chapter to chapter, it appears significant. Similar things, by contrast, tend to recede into the background.

Variables, then, have the potential to add interesting dimensions to your book's claims. However, they also risk detracting from your book. For instance, they might divert attention from more important variables, make it difficult to follow important threads from chapter to chapter, or cause the reader to wonder why you've changed focus.

In this step, you'll assess whether your variables add more than they detract and make plans to revise your chapters based on what you find.

To illustrate this work, consider the book about the urban South. Because there are so many variables, whatever main lessons the author wants her reader to take from her book might fail to stand out from the ever-shifting frame. Historians of the urban South might find all of the material in the individual chapters interesting, but the book's main claim(s) might get lost.

Revising the book with parallelism in mind will help this author produce a more cohesive and coherent book. If she holds at least one variable constant, she can reevaluate her chapters to discover whether the variables/non-parallelisms help or hinder her argument.

Since her book seems to be making a chronological argument (this will be her book's organizing principle and therefore its main variable), we recommend that this author try to control for at least one of the other variables. She should consider revising the chapters' geographical scope by narrowing her focus or adding new material (keeping in mind her time constraints).

Notice, for instance, that many of her chapters center on Tennessee, so she might consider revising her chapters to hold that place constant. In this version of the book, the Wonder Bread factory could become her central case study. She would then probably eliminate chapter 5 altogether and reduce the scope of chapters 3 and 6 to focus primarily on Tennessee, rather than on three states or the region. We might even suggest that she reorder her chapters such that the opening day of the Wonder Bread factory opens the book and the closing concludes it. (Note that she could also hold place constant by revising all chapters to be multi-sited; however, we would strongly advise against this idea because it would likely require years of additional research and potentially also thousands of dollars in research trips to archives and conferences. This is simply not feasible for most academic monograph authors.)

**REVISED SCOPE OF *THE URBAN SOUTH: A LABOR HISTORY*, HOLDING PLACE CONSTANT**

| | |
|---|---|
| Chapter ~~2~~1 snapshot: | The opening day of the Wonder Bread factory in Memphis, 1921, told through eyewitness testimony and newspapers |
| Chapter ~~1~~2 snapshot: | Social conditions of factory laborers in the urban South, 1900–1950, told through historical sources |
| Chapter 3 snapshot: | Legal history of manufacturing labor contracts in Tennessee, ~~Arkansas, and Louisiana~~ 1910–1943 |
| Chapter 4 snapshot: | Governmental interventions in Tennessee to protect workers' rights, post-1923, told through historical sources |
| ~~Chapter 5 snapshot:~~ | ~~Ground-up labor union organization in Orleans parish, 1945–1950, told through oral history~~ |
| Chapter ~~6~~5 snapshot: | Interstate highway system's impact on labor conditions in ~~the urban South~~ Tennessee post-1965, told through businesses' incident reports and internal memos |
| Coda snapshot: | The Wonder Bread factory closing in 2012 |

We can tell that controlling for Tennessee makes the telescoping geographical scope (city, state, region) much more manageable for her reader. The book as a whole no longer looks like a hodgepodge of cases tied together by their superficial relationship to labor in the urban South. Instead, it feels more intentional (because it is).

Notice, though, what this change does to the book. If the author's intent is really to make claims about the early twentieth-century labor history of the *urban South* (and not a labor history of *Tennessee*), she will need to ask herself whether the narrower focus actually allows her to make these larger claims. She will now need to return to chapter 1 of this workbook to either narrow her scope or explain how this evidence base allows her to answer such a broad question. She should also review and revise her book questions (if necessary) and then reflect on this chapter's work to make sure these new chapters allow her to fully answer the questions.

In other words, she will need to answer this question: "How does telling the story of the Wonder Bread Factory (and Memphis, Tennessee) help us understand the labor history of the urban South as a whole?" If she still believes her book's scope is "the urban South," she will need a compelling answer to this question. She will also have to thread this discussion throughout her chapters. Alternatively, she could expand her scope to include research on other states, but she will need to seriously consider whether she has the time and resources to do this.

Variables and their effect can be difficult to grasp, so let's consider another example: the book about musicians and the pay-to-play model. Here's a summarized version of its chapter snapshots:

## SOCIOLOGY/ETHNOMUSICOLOGY

| | |
|---|---|
| Chapter 1 snapshot: | Background of how the pay-to-play model became dominant and its impact using historical sources and interviews (with musicians and club owners), primarily focusing on 6 major metropolitan US cities, with an eye to differences between genre (1920–2005) |
| Chapter 2 snapshot: | Individual responses of 26 jazz musicians with varying professional aspirations in 5 main US sites (large urban to small town), told through participant observation and personal interviews, 2007–2009 |
| Chapter 3 snapshot: | The practices of 3 amateur rock groups with no professional aspirations navigating the policies of Los Angeles's Whiskey a Go Go, through observation of band practices, live performances, and recorded interviews, 2008–2013 |
| Chapter 4 snapshot: | Practices and outcomes of 12 hopeful professional country and pop singers in Nashville, through observation of band practices, live performances, and recorded interviews, 2009–2015 |
| Chapter 5 snapshot: | How social media influencers intervened in the pay-to-play model and what types of content proved most effective for which audience/genre, told through analyses and metrics of posts plus participant interviews, 2015–2020 |
| Chapter 6 snapshot: | "Disruption" of pay-to-play system during COVID-19 pandemic, rise of alternative platforms (Spotify, YouTube, livestreaming), and their effects, told through published platform information (fees, royalties), participant interviews, industry news sources, and participant observation |

When we looked for variables and constants, we noticed that one of the main constants is evidence type—many of the chapters mobilize interviews, and several focus on musicians themselves. Here are the variables we found, ignoring the first chapter (whose function is to present background):

- Musical genre
- Number of individuals
- Time period/chronology
- Geographical location/scope
- Professional nature of subject
- Positionality of actors
- Process under consideration

And here's how the author might reflect on two of these variables:

## MUSICIANS AND THE PAY-TO-PLAY MODEL

| Variable: | Musical genre |
|---|---|
| How the variable plays out across chapters: | Chapters 2, 3, and 4 examine **one** genre each (jazz, rock, and pop/country), while chapters 5 and 6 look across genres. |

| Potential impact of this variable on the reader's experience: | The reader might wonder why the scope becomes limited in these chapters or whether I'm implicitly making a claim that **genre** affects pay-to-play response. |
|---|---|
| Does the variable add more than it detracts? Reflect. | I still think it's important to have these chapters broken up. It would be too much material to cover pan-genre artist responses. I will continue to ask myself whether there is, in fact, a relationship between genre and response, but I think genre, time, place, and professional aspiration all go hand in hand. I don't think I need to do anything except perhaps describe why we broaden back out from chapter 4 to chapter 5. |

| Variable: | Time period/chronology |
|---|---|
| How the variable plays out across chapters: | Chapter 2, whose fieldwork I completed for my master's degree, has a narrower and earlier focus than chapters 3 and 4—my doctoral fieldwork chapters. Chapter 5 roughly picks up where chapters 3 and 4 left off, and chapter 6 examines a temporal disruption after chapter 4. |
| Potential impact of this variable on the reader's experience: | In general, readers might wonder why chapter 2's chronology is earlier and narrower. The other shifts seem logical. Since chapter 5 studies "effects," it might logically move forward in time from chapter 4. The shift to how my topic changes post-COVID in chapter 6 also seems logical for my study. |
| Does the variable add more than it detracts? Reflect. | Would I have the time and resources to bring the study for chapter 2 more into the present? If not, does it deserve to be a chapter at all? Could I make my book's main claims without it? In addition to chronology, it also seems quite non-parallel with the other chapters (number of musicians, multi-sited). Reflect on what my book would look like without this chapter. |

Now fill out similar tables for the variables in your book. You can do this for as many variables as you think deserve scrutiny. If you conclude that a variable—or the way a variable plays out in one specific chapter—detracts more than it adds, you have two main courses of action. You can plan to adjust your chapters so that the variable becomes a constant (by eliminating either a chapter or some of your chapter's parts), or you can plan to explain and justify the variability when it crops up to reduce the disorienting effect.

Remember that not all variables need to be eliminated, but those that remain might seem significant to your reader. Remember, too, that your primary organizing principle is a variable, but that you *want* it to seem significant. So, when you evaluate your primary organizing principle (and your secondary organizing principle, if you have one), you don't need to plan to reduce its impact. It should stand out!

| Variable: | |
|---|---|
| How the variable plays out across chapters: | |
| Potential impact of this variable on the reader's experience: | |
| Does the variable add more than it detracts? Reflect. | |

| Variable: | |
|---|---|
| How the variable plays out across chapters: | |
| Potential impact of this variable on the reader's experience: | |
| Does the variable add more than it detracts? Reflect. | |

| Variable: | |
|---|---|
| How the variable plays out across chapters: | |
| Potential impact of this variable on the reader's experience: | |
| Does the variable add more than it detracts? Reflect. | |

| Variable: | |
|---|---|
| How the variable plays out across chapters: | |
| Potential impact of this variable on the reader's experience: | |
| Does the variable add more than it detracts? Reflect. | |

## Step 3: Handling Outlier Chapters

Through these exercises, some authors discover they have a radically non-parallel chapter—often the final body chapter. (We aren't talking about a background or conceptual chapter, but rather a core chapter that differs significantly from the others across multiple variables.)

Sometimes this chapter is what we call a "pet chapter"—a chapter that's significantly unlike the others, but that the author can't bear to cut because they put a lot of work into it, or people have praised it, or it's especially clever and original. Look back at the chapter snapshots for the musicians and pay-to-play book in step 2. We think chapter 5 is a pet chapter. It sounds trendy—social media!—and it's focused on fun case studies. We can easily imagine conference and job talk audiences and readers responding very favorably to this chapter, independently of the book. But that's precisely the point. Taken out of the book's larger context, this chapter is "cool," interesting, and engaging. But within the book, the chapter doesn't support the book's main priorities in the same way the other chapters do. So, while it might be strong on its own terms, keeping it in the book might actually weaken the book's argument.

If you have a pet chapter, summon up all of your mental fortitude and consider what it would mean to cut it. If it has exceptionally vivid and interesting analysis, could you redistribute parts of it throughout your introduction and/or your other chapters? Maybe you could repurpose it as a series of illustrative vignettes, threaded throughout the chapters. Maybe it could open your conclusion or serve as an anecdote in both the introduction and the conclusion (bringing your book narrative "full circle"). Maybe you could even turn it into an article—a book-adjacent publication that will drum up interest in your book and strengthen your author profile for your book proposal.

But don't move too fast! It's possible that your non-parallel chapter can actually be an *asset* to your book. Ask yourself: Does this non-parallel chapter create an important logical shift in my book's narrative?

For instance, the pay-to-play music book's sixth chapter (on vestiges of pay-to-play in the digital realm following the shutdown of physical music venues) might also seem like an outlier. Yet it's also the most interesting chapter, precisely because it's unexpected: we find evidence of the book's topic in an unlikely place. If the author handles the variables carefully, he can use this chapter to recapture the reader's attention and expand his argument, because he'll be showing that his core ideas have explanatory power that extends to nonobvious contexts.

To assess whether your non-parallel chapter is benefiting your book, you can start by asking whether you could connect it to the preceding chapter with a term like "however," "whereas," or "surprisingly." If it can be connected to your other chapters with one of these tension-filled logical connectors, it's likely playing a productive role in your book. If it can't, see if you can articulate a very compelling reason to keep it. If you can't do either of these things, it may need to go. But you don't have to make a decision now. You'll have an opportunity to reflect on this issue from a different angle in chapter 8, and you'll gain even more clarity after you draft your chapter answers in chapter 9.

Reflect on your outlier chapter(s) in the following table.

| | |
|---|---|
| What chapters might strike your reader as outliers? In what way(s)? | |
| Do these seeming outliers actually hide important logical shifts in your book? If so, describe them. | |

You should now have a solid sense of the variables in your book, the degree to which they affect your book, and some preliminary thoughts on how to reduce or maximize the impact of each one. If your book doesn't require any major structural changes, proceed. If you plan to combine, eliminate, or add chapters, revise your chapter tables from chapter 6, step 1, until they reflect your most up-to-date thinking. If you plan to add significant material to your book or draft several new chapters, ask yourself whether you truly have the time and resources to devote to this endeavor.

## DEBRIEF, SUPPORT, AND TROUBLESHOOTING

☐ **I realized that two of my chapters overlap somewhat.**
This is somewhat common and usually fine (as long as you have a good reason).

☐ **I still worry about justifying non-parallelisms.**
This chapter's main purpose is to give you, the author, insight into the variables your book contains so that you can make sure they don't detract from the reader's experience of your book's claims. Readers won't necessarily notice all of the non-parallelisms, and not all non-parallelisms must be justified.

| How did this chapter's exercises give you new insights into your project? | |
| --- | --- |
| What questions or concerns not found in the list above do you now have about your book? | |
| What might you need to think more about as you go along? Which, if any, choices would you like to revisit later? | |

## CHAPTER 8

# Crafting Your Book's Narrative Arc

## WHAT TO EXPECT

In this chapter, you will tackle an opaque but crucial dimension of your book—its narrative arc—by considering the order of your chapters and the advantages and disadvantages of this order for your book's story. You will then use a structured format to trace how your reader moves from chapter to chapter. Overall, these activities will help you see how the book's narrative develops across its chapters.

Note: We recommend that you use 5″ × 8″ index cards—as many cards as you have book chapters—or equivalent-sized scraps of paper in this chapter. You might want to procure them before beginning the chapter.

### Time Investment

Expect to spend **about 3 hours** on this chapter's exercises. **Do not spend more than 5 hours** on them.

### Common Discoveries in Chapter 8

- **Each chapter contributes to your book's unfolding claims**. This chapter asks you to consider how changing your chapters' order would affect what your reader takes from your book. Doing so reminds you, concretely, that your reader experiences your book diachronically and that each chapter contributes an ordered piece to your claims. You'll articulate these chapter-level claims more directly in chapters 9–10.
- **Your book tells a story**. You might have consulted advice that asked you to think of your book as a story or a narrative but struggled to conceive of academic monographs in those terms. This chapter's exercises help you understand this aspect of your book more concretely.
- **You have a better sense of how your chapters build on each other**. The "what changes, what stays the same" exercise helps you identify the common threads and highest-order shifts between your chapters and, consequently, understand your reader's experience of your book. It can also serve as a template for part of your book's roadmap.

### Common Stumbling Blocks

- **You don't have much leeway to consider alternative chapter orders**. As you've been learning throughout this workbook, your book's claims and structure are connected. In this chapter, we help you see how chapter order develops certain book-level stories (narrative arcs). Often these arcs derive from a book's primary or secondary organizing principle, organizing the chapters from "least" to "most" or "earliest" to "latest" (to develop a sense of progression). However, some books—especially those making chronological arguments (about how something changed over time)—have little to no leeway to consider alternative chapter orders. Don't worry if this is the case; at the first "sorting checkpoint," we'll tell you which steps to skip.

- **You have a hard time imagining other possible chapter orders.** This is totally normal. You might have already settled on the best chapter order for your book's story, making other possible chapter orders seem much less appealing. With these activities, though, we aren't trying to convince you to choose a different chapter order. Instead, we hope the activities will help you pinpoint what *does* and *doesn't* work about several possible chapter orders so you can feel confident about the one that works best. Try to approach these activities in a playful spirit!

## EXERCISES

### SORTING CHECKPOINT
If you're writing a book whose main claim is chronological, start with step 4. Otherwise, proceed with step 1.

### Step 1: Describing Your Chapter Order

Thinking about your book and its chapters through the lens of parallelism likely gave you new access to the connections between your chapters. While the previous chapter helped you assess whether each chapter truly fits in your book (and how), this chapter asks you to consider a different dimension, one that can significantly impact the way your reader experiences your book's main claims: chapter order.

As we saw in chapter 2, authors sometimes implicitly adopt a chronological organizing principle (and, consequently, a chronological narrative arc) without first asking whether this order best supports the book-level story they want to tell. Similarly, authors sometimes order their chapters without ever explicitly articulating the logic underpinning their chapters' sequencing or evaluating whether (and how) it serves their book's narrative.

We're effectively asking you to consider the relationship between your book's chapter order and its unfolding logic. To do this, we'll need a high-order view of what each chapter contributes to your book's story. The good news: you already drafted something like that in chapter 6, steps 1 and 5, when you articulated each chapter's topic and claim and some metacommentary on its role in the book.

First, for each of your book's body chapters (not the introduction or conclusion), write or print/paste three pieces of information on an index card or piece of paper: the "chapter topic" from chapter 6, step 1, box 2, and your "chapter claim" from chapter 6, step 1, box 4, plus a brief reminder of the metacommentary you wrote for that chapter in chapter 6, step 5. You can use the other side of the card if necessary.

Arrange the cards in your book's current chapter order (which, for books based on dissertations, might be different from your dissertation chapter order).

Looking at the cards, complete the following table to describe the logic that underpins your current chapter order.

**SOCIOLOGY/ETHNOMUSICOLOGY**

| Current organizing principle: | Each chapter explores a different facet of the pay-to-play model (artistic response to, consequence of, vestiges/legacy of). |
|---|---|
| Describe how the reader moves from the first chapter to the last: | Chapter 2 could be seen as giving a broad overview of lived responses, while chapters 3 and 4 give more specific examples. Chapter 5 (formerly chapter 6) considers the impact/consequences of this model in light of the COVID-19 pivot. |

**YOUR BOOK**

| Current organizing principle: | |
|---|---|
| Describe how the reader moves from the first chapter to the last: | |

## Step 2: Playing with Chapter Order

Now we'll ask you to be playful—to try out chapter orders you might not have considered before. Even if your chapter order ultimately remains the same, you'll have gained confidence about why and how it works best for your book. It's often through considering possibilities and articulating what *doesn't* work about them that we gain clearer insight into what *does* work.

If you already generated index cards, flip them over and shuffle them thoroughly. Deal them back out, face up. This is your new chapter order.

Here's what the scrambled index cards look like for the "pay-to-play" author:

**Chapter 3**: Several amateur rock groups with no professional aspirations navigate the Whiskey's pay-to-play policies. They adopt one of two main stances to reach consensus and divide labor in [these ways].

**Chapter 2**: A total of 26 jazz musicians in several sites with a variety of professional and nonprofessional aspirations navigate the pay-to-play dynamics. They espouse a range of stances and philosophies and have differing outcomes. Some important factors for success seem to be [A, B, and C].

**Chapter 4**: How individual pop/country musicians all with professional aspirations navigate pay-to-play in Nashville. Their professional aspirations constrain their possible responses; nevertheless, they still push boundaries.

**Chapter 1**: Origins, development, and spread of pay-to-play model. Explains how it became dominant.

**Chapter 5 (formerly chapter 6)**: Pay-to-play model's seeming explicit disappearance after COVID-19, when club shows were not possible and free, democratic platforms (Spotify, YouTube, livestreaming) widely used. Nevertheless, echoes of the pay-to-play model still inform these platforms.

Write down the order of the chapters in the "scrambled order" box. Then jot notes to reflect on what possibilities, problems, and logics this order would generate.

## SOCIOLOGY/ETHNOMUSICOLOGY

| Scrambled order: | 3-2-4-1-5 (formerly 6) |
|---|---|
| Look at the index cards and jot notes (logic, possibilities, problems): | First, and pretty obviously, *not* starting with chapter 1, the background chapter, is a problem. Interestingly, this random order kept all 3 seeming "case study" chapters together, just in a different order. The progression from the amateur groups to a mixed amateur-professional group back to the narrower (professional-hopeful) group confirms that if chapter 2 stays in the book, it will need to precede chapters 3 and 4 so that we can proceed from broadest range to two different cases.<br>The position of chapter 5 (formerly 6) feels right because it examines the legacy in a period when outwardly this model seems to have disappeared. |
| What did you learn about how each chapter works in your narrative? | Chapter 1: This chapter develops the history, emergence, and dominance of the model and thus must come first.<br>Chapter 2: This chapter establishes the broader range of possibilities and personalizes the general idea from chapter 1. Since it's a mix of amateur and professional, it seems to need to precede the narrower chapters (3 and 4).<br>Chapter 3: Really the only insight is that it can't precede chapter 2.<br>Chapter 4: Similar insight to chapter 3.<br>Chapter 5 (formerly 6): This chapter illustrates a surprise: that legacies of the pay-to-play model persist even in the absence of live shows. |

## YOUR BOOK

| Scrambled order: | |
|---|---|
| | |

| Look at the index cards and jot notes (logic, possibilities, problems): | |
| --- | --- |
| What did you learn about how each chapter works in your narrative? | |

Finally, imagine that we forced you to choose a chapter order other than your current chapter order, but that you had to try to order the chapters as logically as possible. Write down the order you'd pick in the "forced alternative order" box. Then jot notes to reflect on what possibilities, problems, and logics this order would generate and capture what you learn about your chapters.

**YOUR BOOK**

| Forced alternative order: | |
| --- | --- |
| Look at the index cards and jot notes (logic, possibilities, problems): | |

| What did you learn about how each chapter works in your narrative? | |
|---|---|

## Step 3: Settling on a Final Chapter Order

Now settle on a final chapter order. Remember that it's *totally fine* if it's the same as your original chapter order. You should have a much better sense of why this order is best.

### SOCIOLOGY/ETHNOMUSICOLOGY

| Final chapter order: | 1-2-3-4-5 (formerly 6) |
|---|---|
| Jot notes about how this order serves your book: | This order maximizes the move from background (chapter 1) to a broad range of lived examples (chapter 2) to very specific cases for artists navigating only one (chapter 3) or a competing (chapter 4) set of demands. The end of the book (chapter 5) then reflects on a surprising case—how pay-to-play continues even in the shutdown of physical venues. This narrative twist in chapter 5 makes the book interesting. |
| Are there any disadvantages to this chapter order? | I don't know that there are particular disadvantages to this order—it's the strongest I can think of. |

### YOUR BOOK

| Final chapter order: | |
|---|---|
| Jot notes about how this order serves your book: | |

Are there any disadvantages to this chapter order?

## Step 4: Identifying Narrative Interest

As you reflected on your chapter order, you may have noticed that certain shifts between chapters are more interesting than others. Imagine a set of chapters strung together on a thread of "in addition" or "also": "In addition, in [domain], [this thing happens]." Then one chapter takes a surprising turn with "however":

**Chapter 1:** In [domain], [this thing happens].
**Chapter 2:** In addition, in [domain], [it happens in another way].
**Chapter 3:** In [domain], however, [what seems to be something different is actually part of the same thing].
**Chapter 4:** In [domain], [we arrive at a new way of looking at the thing].

The shift between chapters 2 and 3 conveys a degree of narrative tension that makes the book sound intriguing, and it lays the groundwork for an extension of the argument in chapter 4. To achieve such tension, you don't even need anything as drastic as "however." Instead, you might have a chapter that introduces a surprising or counterintuitive way of looking at your topic:

**Chapter 1:** A shows B.
**Chapter 2:** C shows B in a different context.
**Chapter 3:** D shows a different flavor of B.
**Chapter 4:** E, surprisingly, also reveals B.

The bank of terms below suggests some logical connectors and adjectives that add narrative interest. Take 15–20 minutes to look at your index cards and experiment with adding one or two terms that highlight points of narrative interest in your book. (You might want to put the terms on sticky notes so you can move them around.) You may not find a good place for any of the terms, and that's fine. This is meant to be another playful exercise—you aren't committing to anything, and you don't need to try to write anything polished. Just use this opportunity to envision wild possibilities. If you discovered an outlier chapter during your chapter 6 work, now is a good time to think further about whether and how it adds productive tension to your book narrative.

| however | surprising(ly) |
|---|---|
| conversely | counterintuitive(ly) |
| whereas | unexpected(ly) |
| nevertheless | alternative(ly) |
| although | by contrast |
| but | despite |
| yet | new |
| unlike | consequently |
| different | as a result |

If you identify an interesting turning point—a place where you can add a "however" or a "surprisingly"—that's great! Go back to the table in chapter 6, step 5, and update your metacommentary to reflect what you've learned. As you write your book narrative in chapter 13, and later when you write your proposal and pitch your book to publishers, you'll want to present this narrative tension in a way that shows off your book's range and nuance. What might at first have seemed like a troubling inconsistency can actually give momentum to your narrative.

If you don't end up identifying any major narrative turns in your book, that's fine too. At the very least, you should now have a better grasp of the logic of your narrative arc. Not all books have narrative turning points of the sort we've just described; plenty of excellent books are more interesting because of their organizing principle than because of their narrative arc. When you begin working *in* your book in chapter 14, you might want to revisit this step to see whether you can use it to add interest to an individual chapter's narrative arc.

## Step 5: Laying Out Connections and Shifts between Consecutive Chapters

Now that you've done the work to make sure your chapter order maximizes your reader's experience of your book's narrative, it's time to capture the logical connections between chapters by asking three guiding questions: What stays the same? What changes? What new conclusions do we draw as a result, or what new pieces of the overall book puzzle do we get?

This activity is designed to help you navigate one of the trickiest challenges authors of first books face: narrating the connections between chapters while threading several main claims throughout the discussion. This is a skill you will need to use in two key places: your book proposal's project overview (or short project description) and your book's introduction. Also, much of what you produce here will become fodder for the book narrative you'll write in chapter 13.

**ANTHROPOLOGY**

| Chapter __1__ to Chapter __2___ | | |
|---|---|---|
| What stays the same: | What changes: | Impact/significance/what this move does for the book: |
| Interest in explaining how individuals labeled as parts of "transient" communities define this term | We move slightly forward in time (early 1960s to the turn of the 1960s and 1970s) and across the city (from Venice Beach to Silverlake). | The main difference between these chapters is how these populations position themselves with respect to this term: whereas Venice Beach inhabitants tend to celebrate the term as a marker of full participation in a "hippie" counterculture, Silverlake residents contest this label, which becomes code in news media and political discourse for supposed deviance from the twin unexamined norms of whiteness and heteronormativity. |

Now it's your turn. Lay out what stays the same and what changes between chapters. Then explain how this move from one chapter to the next impacts your book-level claims.

| Chapter ____ to Chapter ____ | | |
|---|---|---|
| What stays the same: | What changes: | Impact/significance/what this move does for the book: |
| | | |

| Chapter ____ to Chapter ____ | | |
|---|---|---|
| What stays the same: | What changes: | Impact/significance/what this move does for the book: |
| | | |

| Chapter ____ to Chapter ____ | | |
|---|---|---|
| What stays the same: | What changes: | Impact/significance/what this move does for the book: |
| | | |

| Chapter ____ to Chapter ____ | | |
|---|---|---|
| What stays the same: | What changes: | Impact/significance/what this move does for the book: |
| | | |

| Chapter ____ to Chapter ____ | | |
|---|---|---|
| What stays the same: | What changes: | Impact/significance/what this move does for the book: |
| | | |

| Chapter ____ to Chapter ____ | | |
|---|---|---|
| What stays the same: | What changes: | Impact/significance/what this move does for the book: |
| | | |

*Want Additional Practice?* - - - - - - - - - - - - - - - - - - - - - - - - - - - - - - - - - - - - - - - - - - - - - - - - - - - - -

Turn to the "roadmap" section of your model book's introduction chapter (the section where the author describes how the project unfolds and what each chapter shows). Based on that section, try to identify the following: what changes between the chapters, what stays the same between the chapters, what each chapter *does* in the book's logic, and what each chapter adds to the overarching book narrative.

## *SORTING CHECKPOINT*

As we explained in this workbook's introduction, the exercises in chapter 9 and later are useful only if authors have concrete knowledge of the claims they'll be able to make based on their evidence. We want you to have words down on paper—whether they're ultimately usable in your book or not—to ensure that your book is more than an abstract idea.

Use this checklist to identify whether you are ready to proceed to chapter 9.

☐ I know, concretely, what I will be able to claim in 75 percent of my core body chapters (that is, I've done enough analysis to know what I will be able to show using the evidence I've selected).

☐ I have at least drafty writing (including seminar papers, conference papers, job talks, grant writing, notes, journal articles, dissertation chapters, and/or chapter drafts) that corresponds to at least 50 percent of the manuscript.

If you cannot yet check off both the boxes, consult the more detailed information in the "Readiness Checklist" in appendix A.

## DEBRIEF, SUPPORT, AND TROUBLESHOOTING

☐ **My chapter order has stayed the same, which worries me.**
You can reframe this thought more positively: you've confirmed that your chapter order works for your book. As you've gone through these exercises, you've gained insight into what your book is saying and doing. All of this insight will be useful as you revise your chapters and pitch your book to publishers.

| How did this chapter's exercises give you new insights into your project? | |
|---|---|
| | |

| What questions or concerns not found in the list above do you now have about your book? | |
|---|---|
| What might you need to think more about as you go along? Which, if any, choices would you like to revisit later? | |

# Producing Your Chapter Answers

## WHAT TO EXPECT

In this chapter's exercises, you'll choose one of your book chapters and explore how it answers your book questions. Then you'll do the same for your other chapters. By the end of chapter 9, each book question will have a set of answers—a one-sentence answer for each of your book's core chapters. This work will be challenging, and it will take a while, but it's essential for grasping how your chapters advance your book's main ideas.

### Time Investment

Expect to spend **5–6 hours** on the exercises in this chapter. **Do not spend more than 8 hours** on them.

### Common Discoveries in Chapter 9

- **You see how all of the pieces fit together and how each chapter serves your book.** You got glimpses of this in chapter 6, but tracking your book's main questions systematically makes everything more concrete. As a result, you might gain greater confidence in the book and its chapters. Here's what one alum said: "Answering the book questions really helped me see how the chapter has to add to the book's argument by teaching a specific piece of it. The curriculum has said this, so I understood the concept, but thinking through one set of chapter answers helped me see how my chapters will have to serve the book, and I can already see in the future how I will play up certain parts of my chapter and downplay other parts that are useful for narrative but are not doing the central work of adding to the overall book questions."
- **You finally start to see what each chapter adds.** In chapter 6, we asked you to write metacommentary about what each chapter adds to your unfolding narrative. When completing the exercises in chapters 9 and 10, many authors report that this task makes much more sense—they realize that each chapter is more than just an "instance" of the book's claims.

### Common Stumbling Blocks

- **Feeling that the work is harder or more demanding than the work in previous chapters.** You are now at the second "peak" of this workbook. The work is genuinely hard—you're trying to impose order on what's likely a huge amount of material, and you're continually toggling back and forth between the bird's-eye view and the chapter-specific details. Don't worry if you struggle. Give yourself time, take breaks as needed, and just do your best.

- **Needing to revise your book questions**. Any time you move from a higher level to a more concrete one, things begin to break down. Trying to match your chapters' answers to your book questions will reveal holes, inconsistencies, and slight misalignments that you will need to resolve to make your chapter answers work. This is normal. Tweak your book questions if you can do it quickly, or jot down some notes about what needs to change. You'll have the chance to revise your book questions thoroughly in chapter 10.

- **Aiming for perfection with your chapter answers**. Here again we encounter our favorite refrain: this workbook is iterative. Do a good enough job articulating your chapter answers (get to 80 percent) for now; you'll revise them soon enough.

- **Continuing to collect terms you will need to define in relation to each other**. Just as you likely discovered a few "placeholder" terms in chapters 3–5, drafting your chapter answers might reveal imprecise terminology. You'll revisit it in chapter 10.

- **Discovering that you need to do more research**. If one (or more) of your chapters is based on new research—not derived from the dissertation, a journal article, or a conference paper—you may find at this point that you don't know enough to be confident about your chapter answers. In that case, take some time to do more research—but don't give yourself unlimited time. We recommend giving yourself one or two research sessions, however you define them (days, afternoons, weeks), to delve into your sources. Then pick up this chapter where you left off.

## EXERCISES

### Step 1: Transforming Your Templates into Chapter Answers

First, choose one of your core body/empirical chapters—that is, *not* the book's introduction or conclusion, and *not* a background/historical or conceptual chapter.

Write down all of your most recent book questions (from chapter 5, step 4) and your answer templates, updating them as necessary to reflect any revisions you've made to the questions. Then draft an answer to each book question for your chosen chapter. If it helps, you can highlight or otherwise typographically indicate your template item and the corresponding chapter-specific concept.

It's fine if your chapter answer doesn't follow the template exactly. But make sure it directly answers the major question posed by the book question.

**HISTORY**

| | |
|---|---|
| Book Question 1 (copy from chapter 5, step 4): | How did the Christian homeschooling movement of the 1990s and 2000s encourage white American homeschooling evangelicals to identify with conservative political causes? |
| Answer Template (copy from chapter 5, step 4; update as necessary): | The homeschooling movement encouraged white evangelicals to identify with conservative political causes [**in this chapter-specific way**]. |
| Chapter _2_ specific answer (Q1Ch2): | The homeschooling movement encouraged white evangelicals to identify with conservative political causes **by disseminating textbooks, children's biographies, and other media that taught a whitewashed and nationalist view of US history**. |

| Book Question 2 (copy from chapter 5, step 4): | What strategies did organizations and networks associated with the homeschooling movement use to push white American homeschooling evangelicals to transform this identification into political action? |
|---|---|
| Answer Template (copy from chapter 5, step 4; update as necessary): | **[This chapter-specific organization/network associated with the homeschooling movement]** [used this chapter-specific strategy] to translate this identification into [this chapter-specific type of political action]. |
| Chapter _2_ specific answer (Q2Ch2): | **Ministry and media companies such as Focus on the Family and Summit Ministries** sponsored conferences, message boards, seminars, and camps that implicitly or explicitly encouraged straight-ticket voting for the Republican Party as an expression of faithfulness to Christian and American tradition. |

Note: The numbering convention for chapter answers is Q#Ch‡, where # represents the book question number (e.g., Book Question 2 would be represented as Q2) and ‡ represents the number of the chapter that's answering the question. So the chapter answer for chapter 3 that responds to Book Question 1 would be Q1Ch3. The chapter answer for chapter 1 that responds to Book Question 2 would be Q2Ch1.

You'll be completing this table in multiple steps. For now, choose *one* chapter. Answer each book question *for that chapter only*. For each book question, then, you will write just one chapter answer. If you prefer to work on the computer, it's fine to type out your answers. If you have more than six chapters, continue on a separate page.

| Book Question 1 (copy from chapter 5, step 4): | |
|---|---|
| Answer Template (copy from chapter 5, step 4; update as necessary): | |
| Chapter 1 answer (Q1Ch1): | |
| Chapter 2 answer (Q1Ch2): | |
| Chapter 3 answer (Q1Ch3): | |

| Chapter 4 answer (Q1Ch4): | |
| --- | --- |
| Chapter 5 answer (Q1Ch5): | |
| Chapter 6 answer (Q1Ch6): | |

| Book Question 2 (copy from chapter 5, step 4): | |
| --- | --- |
| Answer Template (copy from chapter 5, step 4; update as necessary): | |
| Chapter 1 answer (Q2Ch1): | |
| Chapter 2 answer (Q2Ch2): | |
| Chapter 3 answer (Q2Ch3): | |
| Chapter 4 answer (Q2Ch4): | |
| Chapter 5 answer (Q2Ch5): | |

| Chapter 6 answer (Q2Ch6): | |
| --- | --- |

| Book Question 3 (copy from chapter 5, step 4): | |
| --- | --- |
| Answer Template (copy from chapter 5, step 4; update as necessary): | |
| Chapter 1 answer (Q3Ch1): | |
| Chapter 2 answer (Q3Ch2): | |
| Chapter 3 answer (Q3Ch3): | |
| Chapter 4 answer (Q3Ch4): | |
| Chapter 5 answer (Q3Ch5): | |
| Chapter 6 answer (Q3Ch6): | |

Congratulations! You have your first set of chapter answers!

## Step 2: Collecting Your Key Terms

Before you write the remaining chapter answers, it's a good idea to spend some time assessing the fit between your questions and answers. Essentially, we're treating this first set of chapter answers as a trial run to see how well your book questions are working to generate answers. First, let's focus on key terms in the questions—and specifically, terms that get translated into chapter-specific concepts. We called these terms "bucket concepts" in chapter 3, step 4, because they implicitly contain a group of more specific terms.

Look back at the table in step 1 and identify the key terms in your book questions and the corresponding chapter-level concepts. The table below illustrates what you might see. You're going to copy these terms down in another table in a moment, so there's no need to write anything for now.

### HISTORY

Table from step 1:

| Book Question 2 (copy from chapter 5, step 4): | What strategies did **organizations and networks** associated with the homeschooling movement use to push white American homeschooling evangelicals to transform this identification into <u>political action</u>? |
|---|---|
| Answer Template (copy from chapter 5, step 4): | **[This chapter-specific organization/network associated with the homeschooling movement]** [used this chapter-specific strategy] to translate this identification into [<u>this chapter-specific type of political action</u>]. |
| Chapter 2 answer (Q2Ch2): | **Ministry and media companies such as Focus on the Family and Summit Ministries** sponsored conferences, message boards, seminars, and camps that implicitly or explicitly encouraged <u>straight-ticket voting for the Republican Party</u> as an expression of faithfulness to Christian and American tradition. |

Next, copy each key term from your book answers into the table below. Then add the answer templates and the corresponding chapter-specific terms from your chapter answers. Here's an example:

| Where found | Term |
|---|---|
| Book Question 2: | Strategies (to transform identification into action) |
| Answer Template: | This chapter-specific strategy |
| Q2Ch2: | Sponsored conferences, message boards, seminars, and camps |

| Where found | Term |
|---|---|
| Book Question 2: | Organizations and networks associated with the homeschooling movement |
| Answer Template: | This chapter-specific organization/network |
| Q2Ch2: | Ministry and media companies such as Focus on the Family and Summit Ministries |

| Where found | Term |
|---|---|
| Book Question 2: | Political action |
| Answer Template: | This chapter-specific political action |
| Q2Ch2: | Straight-ticket voting for the Republican Party |

If you find a term in your answer that doesn't quite correspond to your book question, or, conversely, if you find a book question "bucket concept" that isn't yet reflected in your templatized answer or chapter answer, that's fine. Write down *everything* you think might be a bucket concept for the moment.

Note: You're still working with chapter answers for just one chapter. If it's chapter 2, for example, fill in *only the rows labeled Ch2.* You'll fill in the other rows in a later step.

Now complete the tables. If you run out of space, continue on a separate page.

| Where found | Term |
|---|---|
| Book Question __: | |
| Answer Template: | |
| Q__Ch1: | |
| Q__Ch2: | |
| Q__Ch3: | |
| Q__Ch4: | |
| Q__Ch5: | |
| Q__Ch6: | |
| Notes (complete in steps 3 and 4): | |

| Where found | Term |
|---|---|
| Book Question ___: | |
| Answer Template: | |
| Q__Ch1: | |
| Q__Ch2: | |
| Q__Ch3: | |
| Q__Ch4: | |
| Q__Ch5: | |
| Q__Ch6: | |
| Notes (complete in steps 3 and 4): | |

| Where found | Term |
|---|---|
| Book Question ___: | |

| | |
|---|---|
| Answer Template: | |
| Q__Ch1: | |
| Q__Ch2: | |
| Q__Ch3: | |
| Q__Ch4: | |
| Q__Ch5: | |
| Q__Ch6: | |
| Notes (complete in steps 3 and 4): | |

| Where found | Term |
|---|---|
| Book Question ___: | |
| Answer Template: | |
| Q__Ch1: | |

| Q__Ch2: | |
|---|---|
| Q__Ch3: | |
| Q__Ch4: | |
| Q__Ch5: | |
| Q__Ch6: | |
| Notes (complete in steps 3 and 4): | |

| Where found | Term |
|---|---|
| Book Question ___: | |
| Answer Template: | |
| Q__Ch1: | |
| Q__Ch2: | |
| Q__Ch3: | |

| Q_Ch4: | |
|---|---|
| Q_Ch5: | |
| Q_Ch6: | |
| Notes (complete in steps 3 and 4): | |

| Where found | Term |
|---|---|
| Book Question ___: | |
| Answer Template: | |
| Q_Ch1: | |
| Q_Ch2: | |
| Q_Ch3: | |
| Q_Ch4: | |
| Q_Ch5: | |

| Q__Ch6: | |
|---|---|
| Notes (complete in steps 3 and 4): | |

| Where found | Term |
|---|---|
| Book Question ___: | |
| Answer Template: | |
| Q__Ch1: | |
| Q__Ch2: | |
| Q__Ch3: | |
| Q__Ch4: | |
| Q__Ch5: | |
| Q__Ch6: | |

| Notes (complete in steps 3 and 4): | |
|---|---|
| | |

| Where found | Term |
|---|---|
| Book Question ___: | |
| Answer Template: | |
| Q__Ch1: | |
| Q__Ch2: | |
| Q__Ch3: | |
| Q__Ch4: | |
| Q__Ch5: | |
| Q__Ch6: | |

| Notes (complete in steps 3 and 4): | |
|---|---|
| | |

## Step 3: Scrutinizing Your Terms

Now you'll look closely at these terms. For each set, ask yourself: Is [chapter-specific word or phrase] *really* an example of [book question bucket concept]?

In the cases above, you'd ask:

1. Is running conferences, message boards, seminars, and camps *really* an example of a strategy to transform identification into action?
2. Are ministry and media companies such as Focus on the Family and Summit Ministries *really* examples of organizations or networks associated with the homeschooling movement?
3. Is voting for the Republican Party *really* an example of political action?

Make notes about what you find in the space in the designated row. The answers to some of your questions might be obvious (see #3); others might seem nonsensical.

Make any quick revisions that occur to you. In chapter 10, you'll revise again when you compare this chapter's terms to those of other chapters.

### HISTORY

| Where found | Term |
|---|---|
| Book Question 2: | Political action |
| Answer Template: | This chapter-specific political action |
| Q2Ch2: | Voting for the Republican Party |
| Notes: | Yes, I am sure that "voting for the Republican Party" is an example of political action. |

### CULTURAL HISTORY

| Where found | Term |
|---|---|
| Book Question 2: | Performance art |
| Answer Template: | This chapter-specific example of performance art |
| Q2Ch1: | Protest songs |
| Notes: | Actually, "protest songs" are performances, but "performance art" usually involves one or more nonmusical performers. Maybe I could change my book question term to "performances" or "music and performance art"? |

## Step 4: Noticing and Revising

Finally, you'll read your chapter answers one last time with an eye toward ensuring that they both capture what you mean to show in the individual chapters and align themselves reasonably well with the story you're telling. You'll pay particular attention to **actors**, **actions**, and **directionality** (who is carrying out the action and who is being acted upon).

You will be working one chapter at a time.

For this step, you can mark up the table you completed in step 1. Alternatively, you can type out your book questions and the chapter's worth of answers you just produced. Double- (or even triple-) space your book questions and chapter answers and print them out. Or use a tablet with a writing utensil. What's important is that you have a way to circle, underline, and draw arrows.

### MARK UP AND SCRUTINIZE ACTIONS

Underline the *central action* of each book question. Ask yourself: What action is taking place here?

Then do the same for each chapter answer. Ask yourself: Is the action essentially the same, or at least parallel, in each question/answer pairing? If not, why not?

Use the following formula and examples to guide you.

**Formula question for scrutinizing actions**: Is [chapter answer example] *really* a type of [book question verb]? (Think especially about the implied activity and passivity of verbs and their directionality.)

| | |
|---|---|
| Simplified book question: | How did women in 1950s Idaho **secure rights** for themselves? |
| Simplified chapter answer: | Women in church groups **met with** each other to **plan**. |
| Scrutinizing actions: | Are meeting up and planning really examples of securing rights? |
| Notes: | Meeting and planning seem less focused on the accomplishment implied by "securing." Should the book question verb become broader to allow "meeting and planning," or should the chapter answer make a different statement that better outlines the accomplishments of these women? |

| | |
|---|---|
| Simplified book question: | What strategies do K–4 students on the autism spectrum use to **contest** teasing in a variety of school settings? |
| Simplified chapter answer: | K–4 students on the autism spectrum often **defer** to adults during recess. |
| Scrutinizing actions: | Is **deferring** really an example of **contesting**? |
| Notes: | Contesting usually implies a certain degree of activity, while deferring seems to imply passivity. Is there a way to make the book question verb more flexible in terms of activity and passivity (like "respond to," which could be active or passive)? Or should the phrase "in ways both active and passive" be added? |

### MARK UP AND SCRUTINIZE ACTORS

Draw a box around the *actor* of each book question and chapter answer. In other words, identify who's doing the action. Then ask yourself:

1. Is the actor also the grammatical subject of the sentence? If not, how could you make it so?
2. Are the actors the same (or similar, or parallel) in each paired book question and chapter answer?

| Book question: | What changing notions of "family" emerge in fictional works by Franco-phone West and Central African authors? |
|---|---|
| Chapter answer: | Marguerite Abouet redefines family to include friend networks in the *Aya de Yopougon* graphic novel series. |
| Scrutinizing actors: | The actor of the book question is "notions of 'family,'" while the actor of the chapter answer is the author. |
| Notes: | Should the chapter answer be reworded to center the notion of family? For instance: Marguerite Abouet's notion of family as an extended friend network emerges in the *Aya de Yopougon* graphic novel series. |

As part of this exercise, you may also find it useful to underline the direct object of the action, if there is one.

As you go through this noticing exercise and the revision activities that you're about to start, you may find yourself wanting to revise your book questions. This is great! It's a normal and expected part of working on chapter answers. Do the revision if you can complete it relatively efficiently, but don't get bogged down. You'll return to your book questions after you finish all of your chapter answers.

## Optional Step 5: Expanding and Condensing Your Chapter Answers

If you aren't satisfied with your chapter answers—if it feels as though they aren't quite capturing what you want to say or if you feel too locked into the template—try this exercise to see them in a new way. First, revise your chapter answers to be at least 30 percent longer than your originals. Be wordy! Explain yourself excessively! Don't worry too much about syntax, and feel free to deviate from the templatized chapter answers quite a bit.

Now cut the expanded chapter answers by at least half. Make tough decisions about what is truly most important and ruthlessly eliminate everything else. Err on the side of saying too little.

Finally, rewrite your chapter answers one more time: find a happy medium between the short and the long answers.

## Step 6: Producing the Rest of Your Chapter Answers

Now repeat steps 1–5 for every other body chapter in your book. Remember to exclude any background/theoretical chapters, your book's introduction, and your book's conclusion.

# DEBRIEF, SUPPORT, AND TROUBLESHOOTING

☐ **This exercise feels reductive.**

You're right that in this chapter, we're reducing your chapter's essence to one purpose: directly answering (in highly prescribed ways!) the main questions the book asks. Keep in mind that your chapters will certainly do more interesting things. The important work *on* your book, though, involves distilling and prioritizing your book's (and, consequently, your chapters') claims. For now, respect the format; when you get to your work *in* your chapters, you can expand all you want (provided that doing so serves your chapter's priorities!).

| | |
|---|---|
| How did this chapter's exercises give you new insights into your project? | |
| What questions or concerns not found in the list above do you now have about your book? | |
| What might you need to think more about as you go along? Which, if any, choices would you like to revisit later? | |

# Revising Your Chapter Answers as a Group and Refining Your Book Questions

## WHAT TO EXPECT

In this chapter, you'll revise your chapter answers to assess their parallelism and other features, and you'll tweak your book questions as necessary. You may find that your questions and answers don't need many changes, or you may find yourself rethinking big issues. Either way, you'll likely emerge with a clearer understanding of your project.

### Time Investment

Expect to spend **5–6 hours** on this chapter's exercises. **Do not spend more than 8 hours** on them.

### Common Discoveries in Chapter 10

- **A more accurate understanding of your project's concepts and the relationships between them.** This chapter asks you to dissect your chapter answers, feature by feature. As you do so, you'll be forced to clarify your thinking.
- **More confidence in your book.** This chapter (like the previous ones) challenges you to stress-test your articulation of your concepts. Though doing so may provoke anxiety, it's also a crucial ingredient in developing confidence in the project.

### Common Stumbling Blocks

- **Resisting revision.** You'll spend most of your energy on revising, completing several—sometimes overlapping—narrowly focused passes. Try to keep an open mind and resist the urge to scrap your work and start over from scratch.
- **Aiming for perfection.** Move quickly and respect the time limit. You *could* easily spend a lot more time producing what you think are the "perfect" questions and answers. But because this curriculum is iterative (you will likely tweak your chapter answers when revising your chapters in chapters 14 and 15), the returns on your hourly investment once your book questions and chapter answers are "good enough" (80 percent) are infinitesimal. Revise as thoroughly as you can in the hours allotted, address the biggest concerns first, and then move on.

## EXERCISES

### Step 1: Reassessing Your Terminology

Now that you've finished all of your chapter answers, it's time to assess their terminology for consistency. Review the tables you filled out in chapter 9, step 2, especially the notes you took in chapter 9, step 3.

Ask yourself: Are the terms parallel—not just to the book question (you checked that before), but to the other chapters? That is, are they all related to their book question bucket concept in approximately the same way?

For instance, consider the following example. Notice that all of the phrases in the chapter answers might have *seemed* like scales when considered individually, but when taken together, they clash. Q2Ch1's term now seems more like an announcement of the evidence base.

ORIGINAL TABLE

| Where found | Term |
|---|---|
| Book Question 2: | At varying scales |
| Answer Template: | [at this scale] |
| Q2Ch1: | In personal testimonies |
| Q2Ch2: | In the country's urban capital |
| Q2Ch3: | At the international level |
| Author Notes: | Yes, these are all examples of scales that exist in my book. |
| Meta-Notes: | While these are all examples of scales, they're not all parallel. "In personal testimonies" is not the same type of scale as "at the international level." Consider revising the chapter answers to be more parallel or ask whether this is actually a bucket concept in your book. If not, eliminate it from the book question. |

In the next table, the author has chosen to revise the chapter answers' terms to be more parallel with each other.

REVISED TERMS

| Where found | Term |
|---|---|
| Book Question 2: | At varying scales |
| Answer Template: | [at this scale] |
| Q2Ch1: | At the individual level |
| Q2Ch2: | At the national (or metropolitan) level |
| Q2Ch3: | At the international level |
| Author Notes: | Yes, these are all examples of scales that exist in my book. |
| Meta-Notes: | These concepts are now parallel to each other. |

You might discover instead that it's the book question's "bucket concept" that's not quite right. Again, you can ask yourself: Are all of these terms related to their book question bucket concept in approximately the same way? Reprising this question can help you both assess the vocabulary and imagine alternative bucket concepts that would strengthen your book questions.

## ORIGINAL TABLE

| Where found | Term |
|---|---|
| Book Question 2: | In performance art |
| Answer Template: | [in this type of performance art] |
| Q2Ch1: | In protest songs |
| Q2Ch2: | In one contemporary piece of performance art |
| Q2Ch3: | In tap dance |
| Author Notes: | Yes, these are all artistic performances. |
| Meta-Notes: | Note that while the examples are parallel to each other (types of works/media), they aren't what we would traditionally define as "performance art." In fact, the author labels them "artistic performances" and not "performance art" in their reflection. What term might better capture this group of media in the book question? |

Here, the author has chosen to revise the book question term.

## REVISED TERMS

| Where found | Term |
|---|---|
| Book Question 2: | In public artistic performances |
| Answer Template: | [in this type of public artistic performance] |
| Q2Ch1: | In protest songs |
| Q2Ch2: | In one contemporary piece of performance art |
| Q2Ch3: | In tap dance |
| Author Notes: | Yes, these are all artistic performances. |
| Meta-Notes: | The book question's term now better captures the chapters' cases. |

In the table below, write out up-to-date versions of your book questions and chapter answers, revising as necessary. Alternatively, you can type them up, double-space the document, and print it out if possible. You're going to be marking these statements up, so leave plenty of white space.

| Book Question 1: | |
|---|---|
| Q1Ch1: | |

| Q1Ch2: | |
|---|---|
| Q1Ch3: | |
| Q1Ch4: | |
| Q1Ch5: | |
| Q1Ch6: | |

| Book Question 2: | |
|---|---|
| Q2Ch1: | |
| Q2Ch2: | |
| Q2Ch3: | |
| Q2Ch4: | |

| Q2Ch5: | |
|---|---|
| Q2Ch6: | |

| Book Question 3: | |
|---|---|
| Q3Ch1: | |
| Q3Ch2: | |
| Q3Ch3: | |
| Q3Ch4: | |
| Q3Ch5: | |
| Q3Ch6: | |

## Step 2: Checking for Parallelism in Actors (and Actions)

Earlier, you identified the central action and actor of each book question and checked each chapter answer, chapter by chapter, for parallelism with the book question. In this step, you're going to check the chapter answers for parallelism as a whole.

First, draw a box around the book questions' and chapter answers' actors. Within each set of chapter answers (as a group), ask whether all the actors are *the same kind of thing*. For instance, are they all people (maybe different groups of people)? Cultural products? Organizations?

**LITERARY STUDIES**

| Actor in Q2Ch1: | Domestic servants |
|---|---|
| Actor in Q2Ch2: | Mill workers |
| Actor in Q2Ch3: | The concept of empathy |

In this example, chapters 1 and 2 have people (lower-class characters in eighteenth-century British sentimental novels) as their actors. Chapter 3, in contrast, has a concept as its actor. The chapter answer for chapter 3 should be revised—the author, for example, could think about *who* is practicing, thinking about, or talking about empathy in this chapter. If you find inconsistencies, try to resolve them, or make notes about why the non-parallelism is justified and how you might manage it. If just one chapter answer is the odd one out, it's likely a good idea to revise it, unless you can explain how the non-parallelism actually strengthens your narrative arc.

Finally, underline the action in each book question and chapter answer. Within each set of chapter answers (as a group), ask whether all the actions are *the same kind of thing*.

Revise your chapter answers and book questions as necessary to address what you've found.

## Step 3: Noticing and Revising for Directionality

Many chapter answers state that X affects, causes, influences, produces, leads to, or impacts Y. In other words, they make claims that have *directionality*—"X does something to Y." Sometimes the claim goes the other direction—"Y derives from, is influenced by, results from, or is generated by X."

Two problems can arise from directional claims. First, authors can inadvertently write opposing or conflictual statements. This is the equivalent of saying both "X does something to Y" *and* "Y does something to X." If both are true, it's fine to say so, but sometimes authors write conflictual statements without intending to. The latter is a problem.

The second problem is clashing directionality—you express the same underlying idea, but the different grammatical subjects make the sentences' foci different: "X does something to Y" and "Y derives from X." This can lead to unnecessary confusion or an unintended emphasis on the wrong thing.

Here you will check for both problems.

### IDENTIFYING DIRECTIONAL CLAIMS

Underline any such claims in your chapter answers and draw arrows to show the direction of the claim.

| Q2Ch1 | In several influential nineteenth-century American novels, fears about hygiene inflame moral panics about prostitution. |
|---|---|

**CHECKING FOR CONFLICTUAL STATEMENTS**

First, in each set of chapter answers, check your directional claims for consistency. Across the chapter answers, X (or variants of X, or concepts parallel to X) should consistently do something to Y. If you find instead that Y does something to X, revise the chapter answer. This may involve rethinking your arguments.

| Q2Ch1: | In several influential nineteenth-century American novels, fears about hygiene inflame moral panics about prostitution. |
|---|---|
| Q2Ch2: | In numerous nineteenth-century American reformers' essays, concern about prostitution and other forms of sexual immorality informs discussions about promoting proper hygiene. |

Notice that in Q2Ch1, *fears about hygiene* is affecting *moral panics about prostitution*, whereas in Q2Ch2, it's the other way around.

The author should ensure they haven't inadvertently expressed one consistent idea (the link between these two concepts) in conflicting ways.

**CHECKING FOR CLASHING DIRECTIONALITY**

Clashing directionality comes when your logic is consistent ("X causes Y," "Y results from X"), but the grammar of the sentences emphasizes different actors. Consider the following example:

| Q2Ch1: | In several influential nineteenth-century American novels, fears about hygiene inflame moral panics about prostitution. |
|---|---|
| Q2Ch2: | In numerous nineteenth-century American reformers' essays, concern about prostitution and other forms of sexual immorality is expressed in terms of an interest in promoting proper hygiene. |

The basic idea is the same, but the logic is expressed from two different directions. The author should consider revising one of the two statements. Here's how they could change Q2Ch1:

| Q2Ch1: | In several influential nineteenth-century American novels, moral panics about prostitution are portrayed as driven by a fear of unhygienic conditions and inflamed by rhetoric about filth. |
|---|---|
| Q2Ch2: | In numerous nineteenth-century American reformers' essays, concern about prostitution and other forms of sexual immorality is expressed in terms of an interest in promoting proper hygiene. |

Or they could revise Q2Ch2 to match Q2Ch1's directionality. Here's what they'd get:

| Q2Ch1: | In several influential nineteenth-century American novels, fears about hygiene lead to moral panics about prostitution. |
|---|---|
| Q2Ch2: | In numerous nineteenth-century American reformers' essays, an interest in promoting proper hygiene is expressed as a means of making more palatable the writers' concern about prostitution and other forms of sexual immorality. |

Now review your own book questions and chapter answers for directionality. If they've changed substantially, rewrite them below or type them and print them out. (If they haven't changed much, you can skip this table.)

| Book Question 1: | |
| --- | --- |
| Q1Ch1: | |
| Q1Ch2: | |
| Q1Ch3: | |
| Q1Ch4: | |
| Q1Ch5: | |
| Q1Ch6: | |

| Book Question 2: | |
| --- | --- |
| Q2Ch1: | |

| Q2Ch2: | |
|---|---|
| Q2Ch3: | |
| Q2Ch4: | |
| Q2Ch5: | |
| Q2Ch6: | |

| Book Question 3: | |
|---|---|
| Q3Ch1: | |
| Q3Ch2: | |
| Q3Ch3: | |
| Q3Ch4: | |

| Q3Ch5: | |
|---|---|
| Q3Ch6: | |

## Step 4: Reviewing Your Final Book Questions and Chapter Answers

This activity is another moment when we're encouraging you to ask—rather than turn away from—hard questions. In this exercise, you'll take on the role of a skeptical reader (or peer reviewer). Attempt to raise tough questions and/or poke holes in your project. Remember, asking these challenging questions now will pay off later.

In the table in step 1 or step 3, circle the key nouns and verbs in each book question and chapter answer.

Set a timer for 25 minutes. From each word, draw arrows that point to questions or editorial comments about its definition and usage.

**Sample Question Bank:**
- Is this really what I'm studying? Is this really what I mean to say?
- What other terms could I use instead of this one? What are their shortcomings? Advantages?
- What X am I talking about?
- How does Y occur?
- Define Z. Or, what does Z mean?

Now set a timer for another 25 minutes. Respond to the three or four issues you deem most important; then revise your chapter answers and/or book questions as necessary. If your main concerns with your book questions and chapter answers are terminological, use the exercises in appendix D to scrutinize your terms.

Resist the urge to answer all of the questions or get lost down terminological or conceptual rabbit holes. Your goal is to produce a complete set of chapter answers that do a "good enough" job (about 80 percent) of capturing how your chapters advance your book's claims.

## Step 5: Reading Aloud

Read your book questions and chapter answers aloud. As you read, edit them for concision and clarity. Delete any unnecessary words.

Finally, copy the most updated version of your book questions and chapter answers in the table below.

| Book Question 1: | |
|---|---|

| Q1Ch1: | |
|---|---|
| Q1Ch2: | |
| Q1Ch3: | |
| Q1Ch4: | |
| Q1Ch5: | |
| Q1Ch6: | |

| Book Question 2: | |
|---|---|
| Q2Ch1: | |
| Q2Ch2: | |
| Q2Ch3: | |

| Q2Ch4: | |
|---|---|
| Q2Ch5: | |
| Q2Ch6: | |

| Book Question 3: | |
|---|---|
| Q3Ch1: | |
| Q3Ch2: | |
| Q3Ch3: | |
| Q3Ch4: | |
| Q3Ch5: | |
| Q3Ch6: | |

## DEBRIEF, SUPPORT, AND TROUBLESHOOTING

☐ **I still feel like my chapter answers are not quite right**.

While this is the last time you'll be working directly with your chapter answers, they don't need to be perfect to be useful. Their purpose is to state, in a simple and straightforward form, how each chapter answers your book questions. Later, you will use your chapter answers to revise your book chapters (and likely draft some new parts). Less-than-perfect chapter answers can still support you in completing these revisions. That said, if you have *serious* reservations about your book- or chapter-level terms, consult appendix D.

☐ **I'm now sure that two chapters need to be combined (or that one chapter needs to be eliminated)**.

Eliminating or combining chapters with similar claims can ultimately make your book stronger. You may be able to repurpose some of the cut material for standalone journal articles (or other pieces of writing) that will strengthen your CV.

| How did this chapter's exercises give you new insights into your project? | |
|---|---|
| What questions or concerns not found in the list above do you now have about your book? | |

| What might you need to think more about as you go along? Which, if any, choices would you like to revisit later? | |

# Reviewing Your Book's Changes and Tying Up Loose Ends

## WHAT TO EXPECT

In the preceding chapters, much of your work has involved eliminating paths you *could* take so that you can more fully commit to the one you ultimately choose.

But once you begin revising your core body chapters, everything that seems so clear right now, while you're fully immersed in these decisions, will fade. You'll return to a chapter in six months having forgotten why you chose to structure the project this way. Worse, your future self will completely discount all of the hard work you put into eliminating paths.

Consequently, chapter 11 begins by asking you to review and reflect on the decisions you've made as a way to future-proof your plan. Then you'll revise the material that will form the basis for your book's narrative in chapter 13.

### Time Investment

Expect to spend **about 3 hours** on the exercises in this chapter. Because you're primarily reflecting on decisions and revising material you've already generated, **do not spend more than 5 hours** on them.

### Common Discoveries in Chapter 11

- **Your questions and interventions have been sharpened by this work**. While some authors report making significant changes (like eliminating a chapter or adopting a new organizing principle) to their book in chapters 1–10, others describe much more subtle—but no less significant!—changes. Even if your book still looks quite similar to your dissertation or other source material, returning to the work you completed earlier will show you just how much your thinking has changed.
- **You feel ready to accept this book and commit to it**. Eliminating paths means saying goodbye to certain avenues of inquiry. But authors often find that reminding themselves of the paths they're choosing not to take allows them to commit more fully to those they have deliberately chosen.

### Common Stumbling Blocks

- **Fear of commitment**. In this chapter, you're committing to the book project you've been reshaping in the preceding exercises. Committing might provoke anxiety about foreclosing paths you had originally wanted to pursue. Keep in mind that for now, writing a strong book means rejecting options. At the same time, if you realize after a few months of work *in* your book that your book's contents or main claims require you to take a new path, you can revisit those decisions.

- **Pain of loss**. Your book can't possibly do it all. Eliminating paths, while painful, is ultimately necessary to do justice to your book's main claims.
- **An incomplete list of major decisions**. Be as thorough as you can with this activity to leave an accurate record for your future self.
- **A sense that you're missing a thread**. In this chapter, you will identify the major threads that aren't captured in your book questions and explain how they develop in your book's various chapters. This might be the moment you've been waiting for—in chapters 3–5, we promised you would soon be able to capture threads. When you reach this work, though, you might struggle to articulate them. Don't worry. It's likely that threads will reemerge when you undertake your chapter revisions.
- **Worries that the book will be too similar to your dissertation**. If your book's structure and evidence base are similar to those of your dissertation, you might feel that you can't offer a convincing answer to the question of how your book is different from the dissertation. That's all right at this stage! The key revisions might happen when you work directly in your chapters. Or you may have written your dissertation in such a way that it was structured like a book, and the work you're doing now is mostly tweaking and confirming. Either way, do your best to complete these exercises with a focus on making your book the best version of itself.

## EXERCISES

### Step 1: Reviewing and Reflecting on Decisions Made along the Way

Academic books' length is deceptive. It may seem unthinkable that you don't have the space to fully explore every thread you'd like.

But, as we've been underscoring throughout this workbook, a well-written academic book can develop only a few main claims. If you attempt to write about your topic comprehensively—discussing every aspect of it without prioritizing anything—your main claims will get lost, and your reader will feel disoriented.

As contrived as it may sound, part of committing to a solid path for your book is mourning the paths you've eliminated. Unless you acknowledge the loss of those paths, they'll try to sneak back in.

So, in this step, you'll review and reflect on the major decisions you've made up to this point.

| What, if any, major structural decisions have I made, and why do they best serve my book? | |
|---|---|
| What claim, ideas, angles, or topics have I eliminated or de-prioritized? In other words, what paths have I eliminated for now? Why? | |

| How do I feel about these decisions? (It's OK to feel a sense of uncertainty or loss. Acknowledging it here will help me come to terms with these decisions and make it easier to write the book.) | |

## Step 2: Revisiting, Revising, and Extending Your Chapter 1 Work

Now you'll begin revising the material that will become the basis for your book's narrative. First, produce revised answers to the prompt you responded to in chapter 1 of this workbook. Do this *without* looking back at those original answers.

| My book's topic: | |
| --- | --- |
| What my book does in its discipline: | |
| What my book does not do: | |
| Why doing this intellectual work matters: | |

| The main question my book asks is: | |
| --- | --- |
| To answer this question, I [methodology and evidence base]: | |
| Overall, my book's main idea, claim, or intervention is: | |

Review what you produced in chapter 1 and reflect on the differences. If the answers are quite close to what you originally produced, that's fine! You likely have more confidence about your answers now.

| How has your understanding of your book changed or been sharpened by this work? What, if anything, surprised you in looking back? | |
| --- | --- |

## Step 3: Reviewing Your Book's Structure and Arc

Now you'll review and synthesize what you've produced about your book's structure. Think back to the work you did on your book's organizing principle and narrative arc. Review what you settled on at the end of chapter 8, step 1, and then answer the following questions.

| Describe your book's structure (3–4 sentences): | |
| --- | --- |
| Acknowledge: What are its potential limitations? | |
| Justify: Why is this structure best, despite its limitations? | |

## Step 4: Reflecting on Your Chapters and Their Contributions

In this step, you'll do similar work for the evidence base/case studies. Review the tables you produced in chapter 6, step 1, and your final chapter answers from chapter 10, step 5, to answer the following questions.

| | |
|---|---|
| Describe your book's main evidence base or cases (one sentence per chapter): | |
| Acknowledge: What are the potential limitations of this evidence base/ collection of cases? | |
| Justify: Why are these cases the best for telling your book's story despite their limitations? | |

## Step 5: Capturing Threads

Up to this point, we've had you capture your book using the extremely limited forms we call book questions and chapter answers. We've done it this way because most authors of first books (and many authors of books in general!) struggle to impose a hierarchy on their book's claims. Because so much of what they know about their topic seems important, they try to carry too many argument strands across their chapters. Even when authors know they have to prioritize their claims to produce a cohesive and influential book, it's challenging to do it in practice.

The hard work you've done up to this point has helped you identify what to prioritize. But you undoubtedly have more to say. Certain ideas or themes may surface in only some of your chapters, or they might simply be less important to your project than the claims you captured in your book questions and chapter answers. For instance, say you're writing a book about the uses of comedy in West African popular fiction of the mid- to late twentieth century. You can't write this book without discussing gender, but it isn't a book about gender in literature, and you really don't want to get into the weeds of that topic—others have done it better. Gender isn't important enough in your project to make it into your book questions, but you do know how it interacts with comedy in a few of the texts you study. You decide that you'll deal with gender in just two chapters, where you'll be writing about particular novels that play with gender identity.

We're calling such less-than-central ideas or themes "threads," and this step is your opportunity to jot notes about how they might play out in your book's chapters. While you'll draw from these notes as you draft your book narrative in chapter 13, the work you produce in this exercise will help you primarily when you're writing and revising your chapters (what we call working *in* your book).

In the table below, write a bulleted list or narrative description of how these threads play out across your book. Write about as many threads as you like, and continue on another page if you run out of space.

### PERFORMANCE STUDIES

| Thread: | Ambiguity | Relevant chapters: | 1, 4, 5 |
|---|---|---|---|
| Describe how this thread develops in these chapters (list or narrative): | <ul><li>In chapter 1, *ambiguity* appears in my discussion of the role dance plays in everyday Irish life: it is a public and above all social practice, yet one that is highly steeped in individuality.</li><li>In chapter 4, ambiguity reappears, but it relates to the tenuous relationship between certain regional identities and a supposedly unified national identity.</li><li>Chapter 5, which follows a modern dance troupe, is all about ambiguity. The troupe draws from and actively mixes multiple regional styles while also actively celebrating—in press releases and interviews—the power of ambiguous identities in modern Ireland.</li></ul> | | |

### HISTORY

| Thread: | Value, counting | Relevant chapters: | First half |
|---|---|---|---|
| Describe how this thread develops in these chapters (list or narrative): | Though it's not the explicit focus of my book, a major thread that unites my book's first half and final chapter is a larger discussion of how to quantify the value of individuals' lives and, consequently, various governmental and organizational interventions. This thread plays out quite literally in the book's first half, where developments in scientific methods for testing TB and governmental moves to centralize databases meant that national statistics could be compiled for the first time. In later chapters, governmental and public health organizations are able to parse this data more finely along demographic lines, at which point we see the government attaching different literal and figurative values to solving the problem. In the book's conclusion, I show how public health interventions must make a convincing case for "cost-effectiveness" and "return on investment," which effectively ties economic value to human lives. | | |

| Thread: | | Relevant chapters: | |
|---|---|---|---|
| Describe how this thread develops in these chapters (list or narrative): | | | |

| Thread: | | Relevant chapters: | |
|---|---|---|---|
| Describe how this thread develops in these chapters (list or narrative): | | | |

| Thread: | | Relevant chapters: | |
|---|---|---|---|
| Describe how this thread develops in these chapters (list or narrative): | | | |

| Thread: | | Relevant chapters: | |
|---|---|---|---|
| Describe how this thread develops in these chapters (list or narrative): | | | |

Finally, a quick note on the importance of capturing threads. Sometimes peer reviewers will pick up on an interesting thread and recommend that you promote it to the same level as your main book questions. This is especially likely if your book has "gender" as a thread. At this point, you have spent a lot of time distilling your book's priorities (book questions) and tracing how they shape your book's chapters (chapter answers). You can now see that threads fall outside the scope of your book's main priorities: if you promoted one of them to the level of the book questions, you'd have to make sure each chapter prioritized that idea. So, if at the peer review stage you're asked to promote a thread to a book question, evaluate whether doing so would be consistent with your goals for the book. If not, you can push back on the recommendation.

## Step 6: Dealing with Background Information

Think back to the idea that your book is an intellectual tour. As the tour guide, you're going to have knowledge to convey to your audience that isn't covered by the book questions, chapter answers, or threads. Some of this knowledge will be background information—conceptual, contextual, or historical material that you'll have to explain before the audience can appreciate your argument. This kind of information is usually covered in a book's introduction.

In the following box, jot notes about the background information that you'll eventually need to convey. You can ask yourself: What background information must I teach my readers before they can understand my book questions and chapter answers? What is the context in which my book's main claims are situated? If I were choosing several of the most important pieces of context to put in the book's introduction, what would they be?

| Background information notes: | |
|---|---|

## Optional Step 7: Synthesizing Dissertation and Book Differences

Most authors who are writing books based on dissertations find that the exercises in this workbook help them see concretely how their book will differ from the dissertation. Synthesizing this information is useful for two reasons. First, if you can define the difference now (even in a preliminary way, or even if the difference is minor), you'll have a head start on your manuscript revisions. For instance, if you know that your dissertation was invested in examining "genres" while your book traces a series of "firsts," or that your dissertation foregrounded "processes" of migration while your book investigates "outcomes," you'll be able to mine your older writing efficiently for prose that belongs in your book.

Second, you might someday be asked—whether in writing or orally—to articulate the difference between the dissertation and your book. For instance, some presses ask dissertation-to-book authors to explain the relationship between the two works in their book proposal.

Keep in mind that it's completely fine for certain things, or even many things, to remain similar. The questions we've listed are meant to serve as springboards to prompt reflection, not to imply that all of these dimensions must have changed. If you're writing a book that didn't originate in a dissertation, skip this step.

| How, if at all, has your book's evidence base/case studies and structure changed since the dissertation? | |
|---|---|

| How, if at all, has your terminology shifted or been sharpened since the dissertation? | |
| --- | --- |
| Anything else to note about how the book is different from its dissertation forerunner? | |
| What are the results—small and large—of these changes? | |

## DEBRIEF, SUPPORT, AND TROUBLESHOOTING

☐ **I worry that my book is still quite similar to my dissertation.**

Their differences will become clearer as you work *in* your chapters. For now, don't forget to celebrate small insights. For instance, maybe you thought you were working on "migration," and you framed your dissertation around that topic. Now, however, you realize that you're more interested in attending to "diaspora." This might not feel like a huge shift, but it will have a significant impact on your book.

☐ **I still have questions about the differences between chapter answers and threads and how they will manifest differently in my chapters.**

As you saw in your chapters 9–10 work, book questions and chapter answers form the core of your book's claims and help you pinpoint what is central to your book.

Threads, by contrast, are more like recurring themes. They will be present in multiple chapters and might intersect with some of your book's main claims, but they do not in themselves articulate pieces of your book's main claims.

| | |
|---|---|
| How did this chapter's exercises give you new insights into your project? | |
| What questions or concerns not found in the list above do you now have about your book? | |
| What might you need to think more about as you go along? Which, if any, choices would you like to revisit later? | |

## CHAPTER 12

# Assembling Your Book Argument

## WHAT TO EXPECT

In this chapter, you'll tackle a central piece of your book: its argument. Many authors find writing an argument to be somewhere between intimidating and overwhelming. The good news, though, is that we've designed this workbook so that you've been writing pieces of your argument all along. This chapter will guide you to pull those pieces together. You'll also spend time reflecting on the significance of your book and considering which of your ideas you should classify as background information.

### Time Investment

Expect to spend **about 3 hours** on the exercises in this chapter. **Do not spend more than 5 hours** on them.

### Common Discoveries in Chapter 12

- **You have an argument after all!** Congratulations! You finally get to view your carefully crafted book questions as an argument—that crucial and sometimes elusive element of an academic book. We hope the hard work you've done on your book questions has clarified your ideas.
- **You can finally pinpoint the significance of your book.** Many authors find that once they've written their book questions, they have a sense that there's something more they want to say to their readers—some big idea that emerges from everything else. That's what we're calling an "implicit lesson," or a claim for significance.

### Common Stumbling Blocks

- **Feeling overwhelmed at the prospect of writing an argument.** For many authors, the argument is such a momentous and fraught thing that sitting down to write one can produce instant writer's block. You may be dreading this chapter because of bad memories of times when you were told your writing lacked an argument, or when you tried to write an argument but ended up with only pages and pages of notes. Believe us—we know the feeling. We wrote this workbook with the intention of helping you write an argument with a minimum of pressure and stress. As you'll soon see, you've been working on your argument throughout the preceding chapters, and this chapter will simply show you how to make it explicit. Take deep breaths and trust the process!
- **Having trouble coming up with a claim for significance.** We've tried to give you ways to think about your book's significance that go beyond just "tell us why your project is

important." But if this step just isn't resonating with you, you can do two things. First, go back to any old materials in which you've talked about your project—fellowship or grant proposals, your dissertation abstract, conference papers—and check for implicit lessons. If that fails, just skip the step and move on. Ideas may come to you as you advance in this workbook or as you communicate about your book with peers and mentors. If you've made it this far, we have no doubt that your project is significant; it's just a matter of finding the language to talk about it.

- **Not knowing where to start with the scholarly conversation.** This part of the step may feel intimidating. But keep in mind that you're just jotting notes to yourself—no one else needs to see this work, and it doesn't have to be polished or comprehensive. Start with just one conversation and add to the table at the end of step 1 later if you feel inspired.

## EXERCISES

In this workbook's introduction, we promised that you'd produce a strong book argument, but that we'd get you to that point without using the explicit language of argument.

Surprise! You've now arrived. Even if you don't *feel* that you have an argument, you actually do—it's just not in a form that's immediately recognizable as an "argument" quite yet. Later in this chapter, we'll guide you to *assemble* your argument by drawing from pieces you've already produced.

But the connection between the high-order thinking you've been doing in the previous chapters and a book argument is neither obvious nor intuitive. So let's finally define a book argument. We think Wendy Belcher's definition of a journal article argument is a great starting point:[1]

> An argument is (1) your journal article's single significant idea (2) stated in one or two sentences early and clearly in your article and (3) around which your article is organized, (4) emerging from or linked to some scholarly conversation and (5) supported with evidence to convince the reader of its validity.

But, since books are exponentially more complex than articles, here's how we would revise her definition to apply to scholarly monographs:

> A book argument is (1) your book's **single significant claim or idea** (2) articulated in **two to three related propositions** (3) around which your book is **organized**, (4) emerging from or linked to some **scholarly conversation**, (5) supported with **evidence** to convince the reader of its validity, and (6) tangibly advanced by **each chapter**.

Let's take a moment to appreciate the argument-producing work you've done so far. In chapters 1, 6, and 7, you ensured that your book's (and chapters') claims are commensurate with the evidence you mobilize (point 5). In chapters 2 and 8, you saw how your book's main claims and organizing principle go hand in hand, and you revised your chapter order to make sure your book has a compelling narrative progression (point 3).

In chapters 3–5, we tackled points 1 and 2, turning to your book's main idea (point 1). We helped you clarify what your book is trying to say and state your main takeaway in two to three related propositions—your "book questions" (points 1 and 2), even though they aren't yet in statement form. In chapters 9–10, you produced targeted "chapter answers"—ways of tracking how each chapter advances your book's significant claim or idea (point 6).

Now we'll show you how to check off point 4 by articulating what we call your book's "implicit lessons"—the broader significance of your project as expressed to your scholarly peers. Then we'll turn your book questions into statements and pull everything together.

## Step 1: Writing Your Implicit Lesson(s)

Think back to the idea that your book is an intellectual tour. As the tour guide, you likely hope your audience will take something away from the tour as a whole—an overarching lesson or two that they'll be able to appreciate only after you've walked them through the whole thing. "Monuments," you conclude, "aren't just about remembering our history— they're also about forgetting."

We call these lessons *implicit lessons*. Implicit lessons are essentially claims for significance. You can think of them as statements you make via your book as a whole about either the larger implications of your research (for instance, policy implications) or ideas you hope to communicate to scholars in your field about conversations in the field. (Remember that a critical piece of your book's argument is its relationship to ongoing conversations in your discipline.) In the relatively rare case that you're departing substantially from your field's norms in your approach or type of evidence, your implicit lesson might clarify why using this nontraditional methodology is justified and what it allows you to do.

Think of implicit lessons as something you won't explicitly address in each chapter— in fact, to do so would be repetitive (e.g., "and that's why we need to talk about Y"). You may discuss them explicitly in the book's conclusion, but the main body of your book will have done the implicit work of preparing the reader to understand and accept them. They make a larger statement to your colleagues about why your book questions and chapter answers matter. A key identifying feature of an implicit lesson, then, is that it's something your reader won't be able to understand fully until they've read the whole book and arrived at the conclusion.

Many authors capture their key claim for significance in just one implicit lesson, but it's fine to have more than one. You can write these lessons as statements, questions, or sentence fragments—whatever works best for you.

Consider the following examples, grouped with the book questions:

**CULTURAL STUDIES**

| Book Question 1: | How do postcolonial ways of looking (what I call institutionalized spectacularism) define how racial and ethnic minority authors and artists and their works are "packaged" and consumed in twentieth- and twenty-first-century France? |
|---|---|
| Book Question 2: | How did minority authors and artists position their works (and themselves) within a culture of institutionalized spectacularism (falling victim to it, becoming complicit within it, actively subverting it)? |

| Implicit Lesson: | How institutionalized spectacularism erases traces of its own machinations and, in so doing, allows latent associations between "whiteness" and "Frenchness" to evade scrutiny. |
|---|---|

## ART HISTORY

| Book Question 1: | How did hand-drawn graphic representations of Japanese origami that were circulated in the first published origami instruction manuals (1797–1869) participate in a culture of what I term a "folding logic of knowledge"? |
|---|---|
| Book Question 2: | What are the four main ways this folding logic manifests in the larger Japanese culture of the time—both inside and beyond the practice of origami and its representation in graphics? |
| Implicit Lesson: | That embodied practices, apprenticeship, and technical manuals around this art form (origami) constitute a separate but related art form in their own right. |

## POLITICAL SCIENCE

| Book Question 1: | How does a country's proportion of social media "superusers" who are female, urban, and 16 to 35 years old in the three Maghrebi countries under consideration correlate with markers of democracy in the three years before and the three years following the "Arab Spring"? |
|---|---|
| Book Question 2: | What kinds of political engagement do such "superusers" exhibit in their social media use? |
| Implicit Lesson: | What policy interventions stem from this research: why should policy-makers and international NGOs consider funding initiatives to train young women to become social media "superusers" as a measure to improve democratic markers? |

## LITERATURE

| Book Question 1: | How does twentieth-century Northern European Jewish fiction cultivate what I call a "supercommunity spirit"? |
|---|---|
| Book Question 2: | What does this "supercommunity spirit" make possible through literature? |
| Implicit Lesson: | That approaching these works through the strategy of "interreading"—which entails reading the protagonists as both an individual and a community—helps unlock new religious overtones (especially invocations of community) in these texts. |

Now draft your own implicit lesson(s) by answering one or more of the following questions:

- Why does this book's work matter? How do you hope this book will challenge your colleagues to think differently about this topic or change how they work?
- What corrective does this research offer in your field? What gap does it fill? Why does filling that gap matter?
- What lesson about your topic will you be able to explain in the conclusion, but not before? What idea will make sense only *after* your readers have read all of the body chapters?

- What are the implications of the research in this book?
- Taken as a group, why are your chapter answers significant?

| Implicit Lesson(s): | |
|---|---|
| | |

Before you move on, take a little while to reflect on how your implicit lesson is tied to scholarly conversations in your field. Complete the following table, referring back to the work you did in chapter 11, step 2, as necessary:

| Broad scholarly conversations in which my implicit lesson speaks: | |
|---|---|
| What my book adds to these conversations: | |
| Why adding these contributions matters: | |

## Step 2: Turning Your Book Questions into Statements

The work you did in chapters 6–8 ensured that your book is organized around your argument. But what is that argument? We think it's hiding out in your book questions. As a first step toward finding it, you'll turn your book questions into statements.

To do this, you can either answer the book question in broad terms or subtract the question word, turning a "how" or "why" question into a statement *that* something occurred or is occurring. In the latter case, it's the chapters that will detail the *how* or *why*.

### ART HISTORY

| Book Question 1: | How did hand-drawn graphic representations of Japanese origami that circulated in the first published origami instruction manuals (1797–1869) participate in a culture of what I term a "folding logic of knowledge"? |
|---|---|
| Book Statement 1: | Hand-drawn graphic representations of Japanese origami that circulated in the first published origami instruction manuals (1797–1869) participated in a larger culture of what I term a "folding logic of knowledge." |

## LITERATURE

| Book Question 1: | How did twentieth-century Northern European Jewish fiction cultivate what I call a "supercommunity spirit"? |
|---|---|
| Book Statement 1: | Twentieth-century Northern European Jewish fiction cultivates a "supercommunity spirit" through various literary techniques and textual features. |

| Book Question 2: | What does this "supercommunity spirit" make possible through literature? |
|---|---|
| Book Statement 2: | This "supercommunity spirit" allows individuals to define themselves as part of multiple communities. |

## SOCIOLOGY

| Book Question 1: | How do non-computer science major college graduates from various US institutions designated as "regional comprehensives" use a range of networks to find employment in the technology sector post-2008? |
|---|---|
| Book Statement 1: | Non-computer science major college graduates from various US institutions designated as "regional comprehensives" use a range of networks to find employment in the technology sector post-2008. |

Now it's your turn:

| Book Question 1: | |
|---|---|
| Book Statement 1: | |
| Book Question 2: | |

| Book Statement 2: | |
| --- | --- |
| Book Question 3: | |
| Book Statement 3: | |

## Step 3: Pulling It All Together

Now let's bring all the pieces of the argument together into a short paragraph. When we had you develop your book statements, we were aiming for clarity and simplicity: one major idea per sentence. In this step, you can combine your book statements in any way you want to. Add logical connectors; merge sentences; add definitions or details; delete repetition; rearrange phrases for emphasis; change words; simply copy the statements down one after the other—do whatever seems necessary to put your book statements into paragraph form.

Conclude your paragraph with one or more sentences that spell out your implicit lesson(s).

### ART HISTORY

Hand-drawn graphic representations of Japanese origami that circulated in the first published origami instruction manuals (1797–1869) participated in what I term a "folding logic of knowledge," which had four main manifestations in Japanese culture of the time. A study of this logic shows that the embodied practices, apprenticeship, and technical manuals around this art form (origami) constitute an art form in their own right.

### CULTURAL STUDIES

When racial and ethnic minority authors and artists and their works are "packaged" and consumed in twentieth- and twenty-first-century France, they are defined by postcolonial ways of looking that I call *institutionalized spectacularism*. Within this culture of institutionalized spectacularism, the minority authors and artists in this study position their works (and themselves) in a range of ways, including falling victim to institutionalized spectacularism, becoming complicit within it, and actively subverting it. Their efforts reveal how institutionalized spectacularism erases traces of its own machinations and, in so doing, allows latent associations between "whiteness" and "Frenchness" to evade scrutiny.

**YOUR BOOK**

<br><br><br><br><br><br><br><br><br><br><br><br><br><br><br><br><br><br>

As a final exercise, check your argument against the background information that you brainstormed in chapter 11, step 6. Sometimes authors unwittingly end up framing background or contextual information as though it were part of their argument. Does any aspect of your argument overlap significantly with the background information from chapter 11? If so, think carefully about what you actually have evidence for and about what other scholars have already done. If an idea has already been established in the literature, and/or if you don't have evidence from your corpus (your primary sources) to support it, then it's likely part of your background information. Remove it for now, and update your notes in chapter 11, step 6, as necessary.

## DEBRIEF, SUPPORT, AND TROUBLESHOOTING

☐ **I still don't think my argument is quite right**.
Take some time to explore why you're feeling like this. Is there a mismatch between the argument you wrote and what you think you can demonstrate with your sources? Are you attached to a previous vision of your argument that won't actually work with the sources you have? Does the argument sound too simple? (See below!) Does a piece seem to be missing? Does the language need tweaking?
You may find it helpful to go back and review the decisions you made earlier in this workbook. You arrived at your book questions for a reason—because you decided, via significant work, that they reflected your highest priorities and generated chapter answers that you could support with the evidence you have. If you have qualms about your work in this chapter, you may be dealing with lingering insecurities about the idea of writing The Dreaded Argument. Or you may simply need to do a bit more

revision to get it right. Whatever it is, we encourage you not to pause on this chapter for too long. The next chapter will give you an opportunity to revisit your argument and expand on it. Record your doubts and move on.

☐ **My argument sounds too simple**.

Remind yourself that what sounds obvious or simplistic to you may well read as clear and elegant to someone who hasn't spent years immersed in your sources. Many published arguments are surprisingly simple when they're stripped down—what makes them powerful is their ability to drive capacious but focused chapter-level investigations. You can add explanations and details to your argument later, if you want to; what's important now is to have it written down in its most elemental form.

| | |
|---|---|
| How did this chapter's exercises give you new insights into your project? | |
| What questions or concerns not found in the list above do you now have about your book? | |
| What might you need to think more about as you go along? Which, if any, choices would you like to revisit later? | |

## CHAPTER 13

# Assembling Your Two-Page Book Narrative

## WHAT TO EXPECT

You've reached the final activity of the work *on* your book. In this chapter, you will synthesize the work you've done to reconceptualize your book project by producing a two- to three-page single-spaced book narrative that will guide your chapter revisions. You might also use the narrative as a starting point for your book's introduction and your book proposal.

A word of warning: This exercise is much less structured and the writing you produce is much longer than any of the material you've written thus far. When some authors reach this exercise, they panic—some describe it as feeling thrown into the "deep end of the pool." But try not to worry. You've actually been producing bits of this book narrative in the preceding twelve chapters.

### Time Investment

Expect to spend **6–7 hours** on the exercises in this chapter. **Do not spend more than 10 hours** on them.

### Common Discoveries in Chapter 13

- **You've sneakily been writing your book narrative all along.** The work in the preceding chapters forced you to make important decisions about your book's scope, structure, and priorities and to articulate how its pieces work together. Some authors struggle to see the connection between the targeted, limited prompts they've answered in previous chapters and this chapter's much more open writing mode. At its core, though, a book narrative merely asks you to lay out and explain your project— work the earlier exercises asked you to do in short, targeted bursts.
- **You're writing in a much more confident voice.** Because you've asked yourself challenging questions about every aspect of your book, you'll likely find you have greater confidence in the path you've chosen.
- **Several small "aha"s along the way have led to greater understanding of and confidence in the project.** Not all books look radically different after chapters 1–13. These exercises, though, do cause most authors to sharpen their thinking. Seeing authors experience small but significant realizations (some gleefully proclaim, for instance, "I now understand and can articulate what I've been trying to do all along!") is our favorite part of working with authors one-on-one. If, after producing your book narrative, this discovery resonates with you, please consider emailing us at success @dissertationtobook.com to share your insight!

- **Seeing the entire book on two to three pages is refreshing**. Most authors who complete the workbook exercises have written about their book project for years—from the dissertation prospectus and abstract to job materials and fellowship applications. But many realize that producing those earlier documents involved developing and repeating sound bites and imprecise language, which made their way into later documents. This workbook helps you identify and interrogate those sound bites. When authors see their revised and reconceptualized project on two to three pages, it's often the first time they feel confident that they've captured what their book is actually doing.

## Common Stumbling Blocks

- **The feeling that you're being thrown into the "deep end of the pool" with no warning.** It bears repeating here: some authors panic when asked to produce this longer book narrative. While the form is left open to accommodate a variety of projects and authorial styles, we do offer guidance on how to repurpose writing you've done earlier in this workbook.
- **Uncertainty about the format/genre.** Because this narrative's purpose is to support you in revising your chapters, there is no one right way to produce it. So please don't get hung up on whether you're "doing it right." If, in the end, you have a two- to three-page document that captures what your book as a whole does and what each of its parts/chapters contributes to its main claims, you've done it right.
- **A sense that there's something "missing" or "not quite right."** Just as drafting your chapter answers in chapters 9–10 revealed issues about the book questions you produced in chapters 3–5 in a way you could not have accessed earlier, so too will returning to and revising your book's chapters cause you to revise your book narrative, chapter answers, and book questions in ways you can't anticipate right now. All you need to do is produce a guiding narrative that represents your current understanding of your project.

# EXERCISES

In this chapter, you're going to pull together all of your work to write a synthesized two- to three-page (single-spaced) book narrative.

As we stated at the beginning of this workbook, you should think of the material you generate here as a plan that helps you keep track of where you are in your book's narrative as you complete your manuscript revisions. It would be counterproductive to polish your book narrative to the extent you would polish a book proposal, especially since various dimensions of this plan will shift as you draft and/or revise your book's individual chapters. Instead, aim for a book narrative that's good enough to guide you in future work. Revise it quickly, and then move on.

Your main goal is to explain what your book *is* and *does* to your reader and, most importantly, to your future self. There is no right or wrong way to do this, though typically your narrative will be divided into a main overview followed by fuller explanations of the chapters' main claims and the evidence that you'll analyze to support them.

You'll likely find this writing useful as you're preparing your proposal, writing your book and chapter introductions, and speaking to editors about your project. In the more immediate term, you will use this narrative to guide your revisions.

If you want to work in an open format, open a new document and begin!

If you prefer a more structured approach, open a new document and begin by "assembling"—that is, cutting and pasting material wholesale, without editing it—the basic information. Then you can revise and rework these pieces until they read as a coherent narrative.

Assemble paragraph 1: What does the book as a whole do? (major elements of your book's argument and its claim(s) for significance)

- "My book's topic," from the table in chapter 11, step 2
- Argument paragraph from chapter 12, step 3
- Material about your implicit lesson(s) from chapter 12, step 1
- "To answer this question, I [methodology and evidence base]" from the table in chapter 11, step 2, OR material from chapter 11, step 4

Assemble paragraph 2: How does the book as a whole proceed? (a sense of how your argument unfolds across the book's chapters)

- Material describing your book's organizing principle from chapter 2
- Material describing your book's narrative arc and how your book's logic develops from chapter 8
- "Describe your book's structure" from chapter 11, step 3

Assemble one paragraph on each body chapter: What does it do in service of the book?

- For the second and later chapters, start with a topic sentence generated by reviewing the "what stays the same, what changes" sections of the table in chapter 8, step 5
- Material describing the chapter-specific evidence base from the revised table in chapter 6, step 1
- Final chapter answers from chapter 10, step 5

Remember that this is a document *for you*, *not* for editors. Its main purpose is to help you distill and synthesize the essential in a way that will remind you of your priorities as you're revising. Don't spend too much time on it; you can always clean it up later.

## DEBRIEF, SUPPORT, AND TROUBLESHOOTING

☐ **I feel like something's still missing or not quite right . . .**
Your work up to this point has focused on project conception: you've stress-tested your book and produced a stronger, more coherent project. In the coming chapters, you'll use what you produced to revise your core body chapters systematically. This work will be iterative, just like the work in chapters 1–13. You will continue to sharpen your thinking by revising your chapters.

☐ **Where do I go from here?**
Now that you've systematically stress-tested your book project, you'll work to assemble and revise your book's core body chapters to align with your plan. You'll see how the decisions you've made in the preceding chapters result in a more cohesive project.

| How did this chapter's exercises give you new insights into your project? | |
| --- | --- |
| What questions or concerns not found in the list above do you now have about your book? | |
| What might you need to think more about as you go along? Which, if any, choices would you like to revisit later? | |

# Transitioning from "Working *on*" Your Book to "Working *in*" Your Book

## WORK YOU'VE DONE; WHAT LIES AHEAD

Thus far in the workbook, you've "worked *on*" your project conception. You've articulated clear claims, evaluated your book's structure (and chapters' scope), written an argument, and made sure your chapters clearly serve your book's aims.

During your "work *in*" your chapters, your focus will shift to project implementation. Using your book narrative, book questions, and chapter answers, you'll assemble and revise your chapters to fit your plan. Whereas chapters 1–13 contained targeted prompts, exercises, and examples, chapters 14–16 lay out broad steps, ordered to ensure that you produce and revise your book chapters efficiently. You will tackle the highest-order priorities (like logic, argumentation, and structure) first.

By the end of this work, you should have solid first drafts of the body sections of your core body chapters. The exercises do *not* help you draft completely new material (though you can consult appendix E for approaches to drafting material), nor do they help you draft or revise your book's or chapters' introductions and conclusions.

A final note: Some authors initially find the sheer number of steps intimidating, yet in the end report appreciating their thoroughness. After using the broad framework several times, they start to internalize the steps' main tenets and ultimately develop their own (usually less involved) revising practices. If you tend to dislike following such a systematic process, see the advice we offer in the "stumbling block" sections or consult appendix F.

## FAQS AS YOU REACH THIS TRANSITION POINT

### Am I Ready to Draft Proposals Now?

You likely have enough insight to draft proposals at this stage. That said, we wouldn't recommend doing so until you've thoroughly revised at least two chapters to fit the plan you've produced. Here's why: the plan you've produced is meticulously crafted, but it's still a plan. Before marketing that plan to publishers, you want to make sure it's realizable. As we've mentioned, returning to "work *in*" your book will give you new insights that will cause you to revise what you've produced in the past weeks.

### Am I Ready to Talk to Editors Now?

Probably so. If you've taken the work seriously, you likely have a coherent project and a good handle on its priorities. Many projects that receive book contracts were already on editors' radar before the formal proposal submission stage. So not only are you likely ready to talk to editors about your project, but it's probably a good idea to do so in the next few months (whenever such conversations would naturally fall, given your field's annual conference schedule). Laura Portwood-Stacer's *The Book Proposal Book: A Guide for Scholarly Authors* is an excellent resource for understanding how and when these conversations typically happen.

### Which Chapter(s) Should I Start with in Chapter 14?

We recommend starting with two chapters for which you have a lot of material (like a dissertation chapter). One should be a "signature" chapter (a chapter you think is emblematic of your book). If possible, the other chapter should be one you're less sure about. We recommend working on a challenging chapter early so that you can make sure your plan works. Doing revisions this way will allow you to course-correct before you submit your proposal if you find significant flaws in your plan. Caveat: If you're working under significant time pressure, you may want to start with your two strongest chapters, in case you have to cut other chapters later.

### What about Chapters I Still Need to Draft?

The answer depends partly on what you mean by "draft." If you have dissertation chapters, conference papers, article drafts, and notes on which your book chapter will be based, you are well equipped for the coming chapters, which will show you how to "assemble" your material rather than drafting new words from scratch.

If you have chapters for which you truly have no writing to draw from (not even notes!), you'll need to produce some writing before the next three chapters will be useful. We recommend that authors begin with close readings and analysis of primary sources. For a range of specific strategies for producing new writing, see appendix E. After drafting many such analyses, you'll have enough material either to produce what we call a "chapter collage" or to use the lesson on revising a chapter collage into a more coherent draft.

### When Should I Plan to Draft My Book Introduction?

The answer depends on personal preference and working style. Katelyn tends to wait to draft her introduction until after the chapters are done because doing so ensures that she captures the book's *actual* investments and outlines the final claims the chapters will make. Allison has noted that many of her clients work this way as well.

Other authors prefer to draft the book introduction immediately after finishing the chapter 13 work to capitalize on the "meta-mode" they've been thinking in. These authors typically revise their introduction several times, often months apart.

Finally, since the book introduction and book proposal take similar (broad) perspectives on your book, a third group of authors prefers to write those documents sequentially or simultaneously (and, in fact, some publishers require the book introduction to be submitted with the book proposal).

If at all possible, though, we recommend you "work *in*" one of your book's body chapters before drafting the book introduction so that you can see whether your plan is likely to work in practice.

## How Long Will Revisions Take?

How long your revisions will take depends on the nature and depth of your revisions, as well as other factors such as the number of hours per week you can devote to your project and whether you regularly exchange writing with a partner or group. We cannot offer universal guidelines here. That said, do not spend more than 12 solid weeks working *in* a chapter without sharing a draft with a trusted colleague or writing partner.

## When Should I Plan to Submit Proposals?

Each press operates differently—some, for instance, won't consider a proposal until the entire manuscript is done, while others will offer advance contracts based on a proposal alone (even without sample chapters). So it's also impossible to offer universal advice on this topic. Most—but not all!—university presses will consider proposals six or so months before the manuscript is complete. The best way to strategize your proposal submission timeline is to ask authors who have recently published with your target press about their experience. Note, though, that authors often receive wildly differing advice—some mentors or colleagues will recommend submitting your proposal as soon as possible, while others will strongly caution you to wait until the full manuscript is done.

## What If I Want to Change My Plan?

It's common for authors to continue to evaluate their book as they "work *in*" their chapters. If you're considering changing your book in a nontrivial way, first review the decisions you captured and justified in chapters 11 and 13. Ask yourself whether revising your chapters has given you new information that now warrants a new decision, or whether you're being distracted from hard work by the allure of shiny new ideas. Additionally, ask whether the change you're considering could be solved using less drastic means. Finally, consider whether you will really have the time and resources to realize such a change. If, for instance, your book must be "in hand" in the next three years, it's likely unwise to attempt a major change such as adopting a new organizing principle.

If, after reviewing your past decisions and considering our advice, you believe the change is both truly necessary and realizable, redo chapters 1–13 to solidify your new plan. Plan to spend about *half* as much time as is recommended, since your second pass on the exercises should go more quickly.

# CHAPTER 14

# Assembling a Chapter Collage

## WHAT TO EXPECT

This chapter walks you through the process of efficiently producing a very rough draft of the body sections of a book body chapter. You'll assemble this chapter from writing you've already done. This writing may be:

- scattered across a bunch of documents (i.e., a dissertation chapter, a few conference papers, notes); or
- contained in one main source (usually your dissertation) but needing extensive structural revisions.

At the end of chapter 14, you'll have what we call a "chapter collage"—what you produce when you copy and paste a lot of material into a new document in the service of new claims, with notes about anything you still need to write. You won't revise this writing (yet); the goal is just to put the paragraphs in an order that makes sense and focuses on your chapter answers. This process is designed to be efficient and selective, and it should produce a messy but streamlined draft that advances the book's narrative in the ways you've decided it should.

Throughout this chapter, we'll be referring to the various types of documents and prose you might draw from as your "source material." This phrase doesn't refer to your primary sources, or the objects you analyze in your book—instead, it means writing that you've already put down on paper (dissertation chapters, notes, conference papers, freewriting, existing chapter drafts, etc.).

This chapter is *not* designed to help you if you:

- need to draft an entire chapter from scratch;*
- only need to do minor, superficial revisions to a dissertation chapter (in this case, use some combination of the resources in chapter 15, chapter 16, appendix F, and your own favorite revision process); or
- need to retrofit a journal article into your book.
    *It's fine if you'll need to draft *part* of a chapter from scratch, but you have source material for one or more sections. If that's the case, simply do the exercises in this chapter on the section(s) for which you have source material.

Your final product will look rough—there will be gaps, pieces that don't quite go together, and loosely related thoughts. But even if the product looks messy, this process is actually an efficient way to get to a rough draft—something that you can revise for argument (in the next chapter) and style.

## Time Investment

We aren't going to give you a specific hour limit for the work in this chapter, because the time it takes can vary wildly. However, try to work as quickly as possible—this is not an exercise that will reward endless tinkering. You might consider setting a time limit for yourself. In our workshops, authors have been astonished to find that they could assemble a draft of a section in under 90 minutes.

## Common Discoveries in Chapter 14

- **You thought pieces of your chapter were more developed than they are.** Sometimes, authors discover that they hardly developed a point they thought they made in their old writing. When they return to mine their prose, all they can find is a couple of sentences or even phrases on this topic! If this happens to you, use the exercises below to capture thoughts about how to develop these points.
- **You don't have as much source material for this section as you thought you did.** If there is much more to draft than there is to assemble, do the little assembling that you can, jot notes to yourself about what you will need to generate, and move on to a different section for which you have more source material.
- **You don't have to reinvent the wheel.** This is a welcome but challenging discovery for authors who sometimes have the urge to abandon their old writing and start over. If you feel this urge, try to resist it—instead, challenge yourself to see how much of your writing you can keep or repurpose in your new draft. In the next chapter, you'll revise the material to make sure it serves your chapter's purposes.

## Common Stumbling Blocks

- **Feeling unmoored by the recognition that you have a bunch of cobbled-together paragraphs that don't yet add up to something coherent.** Many authors we work with have never developed a systematic "revising" process; rather, they typically open their draft and start fixing it, sentence by sentence. This chapter asks you to work differently: cutting and pasting existing writing into a new "chapter collage" document, which will be messy. If this way of working departs drastically from your normal revision strategies, it will probably feel uncomfortable. But in this workbook's next chapter, you'll have plenty of time to work on logically sequencing your ideas and revising your argumentation.
- **Getting invested in the source material's arguments and prose.** When we read, we tend to feel attached to what the writing says. In your chapter 14 work, though, it's important to cultivate "double vision" when you look at your project: understand what you have on the page and simultaneously consider how it might serve your current vision for your chapter. If it helps, remind yourself that the point of this workbook chapter is *not* to revise your old writing. It's to efficiently mine your old writing for paragraphs that will be useful in your new chapter.
- **Seeing a lot of "problems" or being frustrated by your old writing.** Many authors we work with become frustrated when reading their old writing; often, as they read, their inner critic shouts, "What was I even trying to say here?!" or "Why did I spend six paragraphs summarizing the history of [concept]?" If this sounds like your experience,

take it as a sign of your increased scholarly maturity! Then remind yourself of this exercise's purpose: not to make judgments about the quality of your writing or to revise anything, but rather to assemble a chapter quickly. You will thoroughly assess and revise the prose in a later pass.

- **Bristling at the number of steps**. About 15 percent of the authors we work with self-identify as resisting structure, steps, and rules, generally speaking. If you identify this way, try skimming through the steps (to understand the broad arc of the work), even if you ultimately choose not to complete the exercises as written. If the sheer number of steps initially feels overwhelming, start slowly and work through them little by little.

## EXERCISES

### Step 1: Gathering Your Materials

Decide which chapter you're going to assemble. Then collect the materials you'll need for this step:

- Book questions and chapter answers for the chapter in question
- Notes about threads that appear in this chapter from chapter 11, step 5
- The other work you completed in chapters 1–13 of this workbook—especially what you produced in chapters 6, 11, 12, and 13
- A good idea of the cases you will examine or points you will make and in what order (see especially the work you completed in chapter 6)
- All of the writing that you could draw from to produce this book chapter, including dissertation chapter(s), conference papers, notes, etc.

### Step 2: Using Your Chapter Answers to Produce a Chapter Structure and Roadmap

With your materials at hand, come up with a very provisional and tentative list of body *sections* for your chapter (typically three to five sections), whether or not you'll use section headings in your book. Quickly annotate the list to describe what each section will do or show.

A quick note on structure: Your sections do *not* have to correspond to individual chapter answers (though they can). More often, each section will examine a different case, work, event, or moment. As long as the entire collection of sections allows you to fully support all of your chapter answers, they're fine.

Also, your sections don't have to be in the order you'll eventually end up with, but if you can arrange them in a logical-seeming order, you'll have a head start.

Once you produce your list of sections, review your chapter answers and respond to the targeted prompts below. Expect to spend 25 minutes on this exercise; do not spend more than one hour responding to the prompt, making notes, and revising the plan for your sections. Just as in chapters 1–13, your goal is to produce "good enough" work, with the understanding that as you continue to work, you will glean more information that will help you revise.

| | |
|---|---|
| Does this plan for my chapter's sections allow me to fully and completely explain my chapter answers? If not, what else would I need to add? If so, is there anything that seems unrelated to helping me explain my chapter answers? | |
| Do these planned sections highlight the work this chapter is doing in my book? (See the metacommentary you produced in chapter 6.) | |
| Do these planned sections help me foreground the book's narrative arc? (See the work you produced in chapter 11.) | |
| Are there any threads that I need to bring out in this chapter (see chapter 11, step 5)? If so, how are they going to show up? | |

Once you're 80 percent confident about your planned sections, draft a paragraph that will serve as your provisional chapter roadmap. Each sentence should describe *what* you study and *why* in *one* section.

| | |
|---|---|
| Write your section-by-section roadmap, describing what you analyze and why. | |

Finally, try to capture this chapter's overall argument in one or two sentences. It's likely that this argument will draw heavily from your chapter answers, perhaps synthesizing or condensing them—or even just reproducing them. This is similar to the work you did to write the book argument in chapter 12, step 3. It's fine if this argument is provisional and messy; no one will see it but you, and you'll have plenty of time to revise it later. Don't spend too much time on it, and keep to the limit of two sentences.

Draft your chapter argument in one or two sentences.

Together, the roadmap, the argument, and your chapter answers will serve as a convenient reminder of your chapter's most important priorities.

## Step 3: Assembling One Section by Mining Your Source Material

For the purposes of these exercises, you will limit your work to one section at a time. For efficiency's sake, think of the paragraphs as the fundamental "chunks" you're working with.

In broad strokes, you'll return your source material and paste entire paragraphs where you think they belong in the new section you're assembling until you've imported everything that could possibly fit.

Choose one section you'd like to assemble, paste the section heading into a new document, and open your source document(s)—a dissertation chapter, conference paper, or notes. With your chapter answers, chapter argument, and roadmap in hand, skim your source document(s) to locate paragraphs (*not* individual sentences!) that are topically related to what your section studies. When you find such a paragraph, copy and paste it into the new document under the section heading. Please keep in mind the tips offered at the start of this chapter: Do *not* try to evaluate the quality of your writing in your source document(s), and do *not* revise any material. Remember that you're merely trying to produce a very rough draft of material that is broadly relevant to your book chapter.

Push yourself to work more quickly than you normally would—challenge yourself to see if you can get most (if not all!) of a section assembled in under 90 minutes. When we run this workshop live, we typically give participants 30 minutes to port over as much writing as possible. They are always *shocked* by how much they can accomplish in this limited time. In fact, several always say that, left to their own devices, they would have spent a full week on this step alone!

Here are a few additional principles to guide you:

**Do**

- Pull any and all paragraphs from your source material that are in any way topically related to your section.

- Try to get the paragraphs you're pasting in a relatively logical(-ish) order in your new section.
- Jot notes about new paragraphs that you think you'll need to write (no more than 3 minutes per paragraph).

**Don't**
- Pull over individual sentences.
- Pull over every single paragraph from your dissertation in the exact same order. (If you find yourself doing this, your chapter might only need superficial changes, not structural revisions. If that's the case, you can skip to the activities in chapters 15 and 16.)
- Obsess over the logical order of paragraphs in your new section.
- Be concerned about whether you've already copied and pasted a paragraph—chapter 15 will give you a way to keep track of everything.
- Stop to write new material.
- Revise anything—*seriously!*
- Get sucked into the logic (or lack thereof) of your source material. Remember: you're constructing this section on its own terms! When in doubt, revisit your chapter roadmap and/or book questions/chapter answers and ask: What work does this section need to do in service of my chapter/book?

### Step 4: Making Notes and Filling Gaps

If you discover holes in your section that you know you will need to fill, you can either jot notes to yourself or do a quick "brain dump" to provisionally flesh out that material.

If you decide to do a "brain dump," spend no more than 25 minutes getting your ideas down quickly and move on. Now is not the time to produce compelling prose or revise anything you write.

### Step 5: Repeating Steps 3–4 for Each Section

For every additional section that will be based on source material, repeat the same steps. You can skip the chapter's introduction and conclusion for now. Your goal is to assemble as much of your "chapter collage" as possible given the source material you have.

## DEBRIEF, SUPPORT, AND TROUBLESHOOTING

Congratulations! You now have a "chapter collage." That is, you have a bunch of paragraphs (and perhaps notes about what's missing) that are loosely related to your chapter's main topic and points.

If your chapter collage is complete—that is, if you have paragraphs pasted in each section that cover the majority of what your section needs to do, even if there are some missing ideas—proceed to the next chapter in this workbook.

If you have whole sections that you need to draft from scratch, take some time now to draft these sections. We highly recommend that you try to produce prose from the "inside out"—that is, start with topical brain dumps (or try the practice Robert Boice calls "generative writing"[1]) and close readings of your main objects. Appendix E contains other targeted strategies. Or, if you like to produce prose from an outline, quickly outline the section you need and produce a rough draft. Please do not produce polished prose!

Once you have very rough drafts of each body section of your chapter (i.e., excluding the introduction and conclusion), head to the next chapter in this workbook.

☐ **The prose I've imported into my section mobilizes the evidence in service of a different argument.**

This is a common source of anxiety: authors draw material from conference papers and dissertation chapters whose claims and terminology differ from those of the book chapter they're producing. For now, the discrepancies aren't a problem. Leave the prose as it is, making a few quick notes if you want to. In the next chapter, you'll revise your paragraphs to ensure that they're aligned to your chapter answers.

☐ **This is very different from the way I'm used to working, and it's making me uncomfortable. Is this really going to become a chapter?**

We get it! Many authors we've mentored equated "revising" with "opening a document and making the prose better, word by word, sentence by sentence." If that's how you've usually revised, this process likely feels messy and strange. Know, though, that this way of revising helps you produce *more coherent* chapters *more efficiently*. In contrast, "revising" from start to finish can lead you to spend dozens of hours perfecting prose that ultimately does not serve your chapter's main claims.

☐ **I can't get over how terrible my old writing is. What was I thinking?**

Let's reframe this thought: the fact that you can identify flaws in your old writing is a sign of your growth and maturity as a writer. You now have a better sense of what it means to write argumentatively, analyze primary sources effectively, and strategically deploy secondary sources. It's *extremely* common for authors we work with to discover that their prose had no argument, that they quoted too extensively from source materials (or summarized them for too long), and that large swaths of their dissertation chapters merely stated what other people said.

☐ **Can I use the "chapter collage" method for other kinds of writing?**

Absolutely! In fact, many authors find that producing a chapter collage is an ideal method for producing chapters of your second book (when you get to that point), which often emerge from writing spread across multiple sources, such as conference papers and notes. Note, though, that the "chapter collage" method works in a specific situation: you must know what the article or chapter will claim or show and what each section (or case study) will contribute to this claim. As you have seen, this method also requires you to have already done a fair amount of writing; it does not help you produce new writing from scratch.

| How did this chapter's exercises give you new insights into your project? | |
|---|---|
| | |

| What questions or concerns not found in the list above do you now have about your book? | |
|---|---|
| What might you need to think more about as you go along? Which, if any, choices would you like to revisit later? | |

## CHAPTER 15

# Reverse Outlining Your Chapter Collage

## WHAT TO EXPECT

In this chapter, you will work section by section to improve your chapter collage—the draft chapter that you pieced together in chapter 14. The basic technique is called "reverse outlining."[1] For these exercises, choose one section from the body of the chapter (*not* the introduction, if you have one). The steps that follow will walk you through some strategies for gaining new perspective on this section, focusing on the highest-order priorities first. After completing the full suite of exercises on each section, you can pick and choose from these strategies to find a method that works for revising the rest of your draft. Alternatively, you can use the questions in optional step 12 of this chapter when undertaking future revisions.

By the end, you'll have a complete draft of your chapters' body sections that accomplishes what it needs to do to serve your chapter (and book). Your prose will still be drafty, but the paragraphs will be in a logical order. You will be certain that each paragraph advances your section argument or main claim in both content and function.

### Common Discoveries in Chapter 15

- **You've changed your assumptions about what "revising" entails.** Some authors we work with produce complete drafts from start to finish and revise as they go. Other authors draft their prose from start to finish, then revise it the same way—sentence by sentence. While these methods have their merits, we've found that they tend to be less efficient than producing a very rough draft and then completing several "revising" passes: targeting the highest-order concerns before revising sentences and finally addressing lower-order concerns like word choice. Working this way can help you identify macro-level issues before you spend dozens of hours perfecting the draft's prose.
- **You have only ever thought about what your writing "says," not what it "does."** We're trained to think about our writing through the lens of argument. Rarely, however, are we trained to think about all of the scales of our writing (book, book chapter, chapter section, paragraph, sentence) through the lens of function. Learning to think this way takes time, but it can unlock new ways of assessing and improving our writing. What's more, starting to think functionally can help us understand what other writers we admire do successfully (and replicate those moves in our own writing). This functional thinking is at the heart of a book we highly recommend: Eric Hayot's *The Elements of Academic Style: Writing for the Humanities*.[2] Especially when he outlines his "Uneven-U" formula, Hayot implicitly asks you to think about your writing in functional terms.

- **You can tolerate more messiness than you imagined.** As outlined above, many authors either draft and revise as they go or draft start to finish and then repeat the process for revising. For most, the thought of having an *incomplete* draft (consisting of polished prose) is more tolerable than having a complete draft consisting of messy, very loosely connected paragraphs. For these authors, the exercises in chapters 14 and 15 are simultaneously uncomfortable and refreshing.

- **Prose you might normally consider "unusable" can become claims-driven more quickly than you'd assumed.** If you tend to scrap your writing and start over, it might be because you hold an assumption you've never tested: that revising earlier prose (that might mobilize evidence to different ends) will take longer than just drafting new prose from scratch. Completing this chapter's exercises can show you that this assumption is not necessarily true.

## Common Stumbling Blocks

- **Having trouble with function tagging.** In this chapter, we'll ask you to "function tag" your paragraphs, which requires you to attend not to what they *say*, but to what they *do*—the purpose each paragraph serves in the overall piece. Because this is a new way of thinking about your writing, you'll likely feel that you're not doing it "right" the first several times you do it. In the beginning, focus on identifying broad functions (offers historical background, traces the lineage of a term, interprets evidence to support a claim, etc.). As you gain experience, you can think about function in more nuanced ways.

- **Seeing a lot of "problems" or being frustrated by your old writing.** As in chapter 14, your inner critic may torment you by pointing out all of your old writing's shortcomings. If you want to, you can jot down a few notes about what to improve—but do it quickly and move on. You'll have plenty of time to revise later.

- **Feeling uncomfortable with a different way of working.** Please try this way of working—doing the exercises as written—a few times to get a sense of what it entails. You can keep what works and modify the rest afterward.

- **Bristling at the number of steps.** As in chapter 14, we recommend that you read all the steps, give the exercises a fair chance, and then choose what works for you.

- **Having strong urges to revise at the sentence level.** Again, please trust the process, which classifies sentence-level revising as a micro-revision task. Once you complete this chapter's exercises, you can consult optional step 12.

# EXERCISES

Broadly speaking, these exercises will guide you in analyzing the prose you currently have, revising your section to develop the claims you need it to make, and revising the topic sentences to foreground your argumentative development. You will *not* revise the paragraphs at the sentence level or consider lower-level concerns like word choice.

## Step 1: Assembling Your Materials and Preparing the Section

Gather the very rough writing that will be the basis for your section. This writing may be any of the following:

- The chapter collage, divided into sections, that you produced in chapter 14 of this workbook
- A dissertation chapter that will only need light revisions to become your book chapter
- A lot of generative writing that is in a *loosely linear order* for a chapter you are writing from scratch
- A very rough draft of a section that is in a *loosely linear order*

Choose one body section (not the chapter's introduction or conclusion) to focus on. Review your book questions/chapter answers, chapter roadmap, and chapter argument (from chapter 14, step 2) to refresh your memory about what this section needs to do in service of the chapter and book. At the top of the section, paste in your main idea or claim for that section.

## Step 2: Claim Tagging (Reverse Outlining) Your Paragraphs

At the beginning of each paragraph, in bold and/or a different-colored font, write a phrase or sentence that expresses the paragraph's main point(s). Don't write what you think the paragraph is *supposed* to say—focus on what is *actually there on the page*. These are your paragraphs' "claim tags."

Remember that claims are *your take* on the cases/examples you discuss, so they should be in *your voice*.

Sometimes you'll find that a paragraph doesn't yet make a clear main claim. Conversely, you might find that one paragraph makes two or more main claims. Write down *what you actually find*—the point-that-isn't-a-claim, the two claims—not what you wish the paragraph said.

Below you'll see examples of some of Katelyn's draft paragraphs, taken from a conference paper that will become a chapter in her second book (not yet complete at this writing). You'll find the claim tags in bold text at the beginning of each paragraph. You will then find other notes she's made in the text in italics.

Katelyn says:

1. I hope seeing these real-life examples from my writing concretely shows you that academic writing (at least in my case) does not just spring to life fully polished. Instead, it evolves from a collection of interesting ideas whose main points I am still figuring out.
2. I hope these examples also reassure you that there is a concrete process to follow to turn this messy, disorganized writing into something publishable. In other words, what you see in the paragraphs below is something I regularly encounter in my own writing. I don't try to *fix* my writing at this stage—that will come later. Rather, I just capture what's there. I don't panic or shut down because "the points aren't good," "I don't know what I'm trying to say," or I discover that most of a paragraph is actually supporting a claim other than the one I state in the topic sentence. These are all *very* common discoveries, and you'll fix them soon enough.

| | |
|---|---|
| Paragraph 1 showing claim tag (bold) and commentary (italics): | [**the way the sampled sound and the rest of the sonic environment coexists is significant**] [*Note that this is a terrible claim, but it's what's there!*] The specific sampled bit of Pialat's film, which follows the *banlieusards'* frenzied morning commute by metro and bus into the city center to work, is thematically appropriate for this part of "La prière du naufragé," during which Jean waits on the metro quai for his train to arrive. [*Note that this is where I find my proto-claim*] Here, the way the "sample" is embedded within the larger track is significant: far from shifting the focus of "La prière du naufragé" entirely to the sampled film soundtrack, it is instead situated within Jean's sonic environment. Whereas the original film soundtrack lacks diegetic sounds of the banlieusards' morning commute, in "La prière du naufragé," one hears both the narrator's increasingly accelerating and passionate narration and trains distantly running through the metro tunnels, one train arriving at the station (complete with high-pitched screeching of brakes, steam releasing, and metro doors opening). |
| Paragraph 2 showing claim tag (bold) and commentary (italics): | [**this layering creates a complex dialectic/teleological relationship between past and present**] This audio layering—which will be found throughout Apkass's album—creates a complex dialectic between past and present. The past (represented by Pialat's film) surges from the present, after which point both coexist and comment on each other. While this is far from the only effect, sampling Pialat's film's soundtrack creates in part a teleological relationship between the two moments, suggesting that the present is, in part, a continuation of the past. [*Note: Here, we've lost the connection to time and shifted to discussing space*] Similarly, on its surface, Pialat's film—concerned with the Parisian banlieue—might seem a somewhat curious choice to supplement "La prière du naufragé," decidedly situated in Paris's city center. Here, two threads/readings emerge: first, the narration only coexists with the points in the track when the trains are running through the metro tunnels; it technically ceases at the end of the track, however, nothing in the sound itself indicates that the track has ended; instead, one hears Jean enter the metro car, indicated by the alarm sound signaling the closing doors (technically the first seconds of the second track, "La chenille de fer"). [*Note that this is tangentially related to time, but doesn't get to the coexistence of past and present*] In this way, then, the narration ascribes a longer history to the metro cars running through the tunnel; it reminds the listener that the trains are coming from a farther place, carrying people who began their commute long before. [*Note: Here, we're still concerned with space. So, I think either the real main claim for this paragraph will need to be related to the intersection between time and space, or this paragraph will need to be split into two: one focusing on time and one on space*] Second, using the soundtrack for a filmic inquiry into the "periphery," writ large, heightens this thematic thread for the album. Though located in the city center, Jean, as the rest of the album will trace, is very much still a part of the "periphery." |

*Want Additional Practice?*

Claim tag a section of a model book's body chapter.

## Step 3: Function Tagging Your Paragraphs

Now that you have an idea of what claims your paragraphs *actually make*, you will turn your attention to paragraph function. Next to each claim tag, in yet another color or font style, write down *what the paragraph is doing*. This should be a "meta-comment" about the function of the paragraph in the section. Examples include "introduces a puzzling pattern in the text"; "gives historical background"; "supports the argument with analysis"; "defines a key term"; "discusses some relevant secondary literature"; "oops, seems to be introducing a whole new argument." Some paragraphs may have more than one function; that's fine for now.

Below, you'll find Katelyn's paragraphs from above, with both claim (in bolded text) and function (underlined text) tags, but without the italicized notes. You'll find a non-exhaustive list of common function tags below the example, for reference.

| | |
|---|---|
| Paragraph 1 showing claim tag (bold) and function tag (underlined): | [**the way the sampled sound and the rest of the sonic environment coexists is significant**] [<u>explains and analyzes particular sonic feature of one moment</u>] The specific sampled bit of Pialat's film, which follows the *banlieusards'* frenzied morning commute by metro and bus into the city center to work, is thematically appropriate for this part of "La prière du naufragé," during which Jean waits on the metro quai for his train to arrive. Here, the way the "sample" is embedded within the larger track is significant: far from shifting the focus of "La prière du naufragé" entirely to the sampled film soundtrack, it is instead situated within Jean's sonic environment. Whereas the original film soundtrack lacks diegetic sounds of the banlieusards' morning commute, in "La prière du naufragé," one hears both the narrator's increasingly accelerating and passionate narration and trains distantly running through the metro tunnels, one train arriving at the station (complete with high-pitched screeching of brakes, steam releasing, and metro doors opening). |
| Paragraph 2 showing claim tag (bold) and function tag (underlined): | [**this layering creates a complex dialectic/teleological relationship between past and present**] [<u>meditates on the effect of this sonic feature and ties it back to the album more broadly</u>] This audio layering—which will be found throughout Apkass's album—creates a complex dialectic between past and present. The past (represented by Pialat's film) surges from the present, after which point both coexist and comment on each other. While this is far from the only effect, sampling Pialat's film's soundtrack creates in part a teleological relationship between the two moments, suggesting that the present is, in part, a continuation of the past. Similarly, on its surface, Pialat's film—concerned with the Parisian banlieue—might seem a somewhat curious choice to supplement "La prière du naufragé," decidedly situated in Paris's city center. Here, two threads/readings emerge: first, the narration only coexists with the points in the track when the trains are running through the metro tunnels; it technically ceases at the end of the track, however, nothing in the sound itself indicates that the track has ended; instead, one hears Jean enter the metro car, indicated by the alarm sound signaling the closing doors (technically the first seconds of the second track, "La chenille de fer"). In this way, then, the narration ascribes a longer history to the metro cars running through the tunnel; it reminds the listener that the trains are coming from a farther place, carrying people who began their commute long before. Second, using the soundtrack for a filmic inquiry into the "periphery," writ large, heightens this thematic thread for the album. Though located in the city center, Jean, as the rest of the album will trace, is very much still a part of the "periphery." |

**EXAMPLE FUNCTIONS**

**Broad Function: Developing the Argument**

- Raises a broad question
- States chapter/section argument
- Asks a provocative question
- Justifies the evidence base (especially if it seems counterintuitive)
- Broadens the scope
- Narrows the scope
- Outlines the implications for analysis
- Makes the case that conclusions from a different context apply to the author's context
- Ties two things together (two pieces of evidence, two fields, two ways of approaching a common object)
- Summarizes a key point

**Broad Function: Supporting Argument with Evidence and Analysis**

- Presents evidence
- Analyzes evidence
- Presents and analyzes evidence
- Notes a puzzle in the evidence base
- Generalizes the puzzle to a pattern
- Generalizes from an analysis or close reading
- Connects analysis to a real-life situation
- Narrows the focus from corpus to one work
- Transitions between two pieces of evidence

**Broad Function: Offering Background**

- Situates evidence within scholarly context
- Introduces concept of [X] generally
- Puts two scholars' conceptions of [concept] in dialogue
- Highlights the stakes of the study, given the larger scholarly conversations
- Defines a key term
- Agrees with and extends a particular conclusion
- Disagrees with a particular conclusion
- Summarizes how scholars have interpreted evidence to date
- Summarizes discussions in broad fields (postcolonial studies, urban sociology)

*Want Additional Practice?*

Function tag a section of a model book's body chapter.

## Step 4: Generating Your "Honest Outline" of the Section

Copy the document you have (the prose with the claim and function tags) and save it under a new name (this is very important—you will need to access the full prose later).

Then *delete all the regular text*, leaving only the claim tags, function tags, any comments you've written to yourself, and section headings. Number the tags (or anything that represents where a full paragraph will go). This is your "honest outline."

Here is what Katelyn would be left with:

| | |
|---|---|
| Paragraph 1 showing claim tag (bold) and function tag (underlined) only (prose deleted): | **[the way the sampled sound and the rest of the sonic environment coexists is important]** [explains and analyzes particular sonic feature of one moment] |
| Paragraph 2 showing claim tag (bold) and function tag (underlined) only (prose deleted): | **[this layering creates a complex dialectic/teleological relationship between past and present]** [meditates on the effect of this sonic feature and ties it back to the album more broadly] |

## Step 5: Analyzing Your "Honest Outline" and Jotting Notes

For now, refer to the "honest outline" document with the claim and function tags for the section you've chosen—don't look at the full chapter draft or the full prose of the section.

Set a timer for 10 minutes and consider the honest outline with *one* of the following questions in mind (meaning that you'll make seven total passes over your honest outline). Repeat for the other questions. It's fine if you spend fewer than 10 minutes per question, but don't spend more than 10 minutes per question. Do *not* "fix" what you find; instead, jot down notes for yourself.

1. Do any paragraphs contain more than one main point? If so, how could they be divided up?
2. Does each paragraph make a distinct, focused point that moves the argument forward in a new way? Or do any paragraphs simply repeat earlier points?
3. Do you have three or more consecutive paragraphs that serve a similar function? That is, do you have three consecutive paragraphs that "offer an example of A" or that "present the literature review" or "introduce background on [topic/event]"? If so, ask yourself whether you could combine these paragraphs.
4. Are the paragraphs placed in a logical order? Where are the weakest points in this logic?
5. Does the organization reflect what you want to argue in the chapter? If not, what material should be moved around?
6. Are there logical gaps in your content/argument?
7. Is every aspect of your argument supported by evidence? (Or—more realistically—will it be supported once you have the time to fill in the gaps? Is the evidence you need easily available to you?)

## Step 6: Creating an Aspirational Outline

You should have a lot of notes about your "honest outline." Producing these notes has likely given you ideas about what you need to do to fix the issues you identified. Now you finally get to start fixing them.

Open your document with just the claims and function tags. In this document, revise your claim tag and/or function tags so that they express what the paragraph *should* say and/or do. We call this an "aspirational outline" because it reflects your vision of a stronger version of the chapter.

In the following example table, Katelyn's revised claim tags are in bold text; her revised function tags are underlined text; and her revised notes are in italics.

| Paragraph 1 showing revised claim tag (bold) and revised function tag (underlined) only: | **[Revised claim = what I think I want to show/claim by analyzing this moment: layering the sampled sound (which represents the past) and the diegetic sound (which represents the present) in this moment creates a temporal dialectic.]** [should do = explains and analyzes a particular sonic feature of one moment] |
|---|---|
| New paragraph 2 showing revised claim tag (bold), revised function tag (underlined), and comments (italics): | **[Revised claim = this temporal dialectic is also found elsewhere/ more generally on the album.]** [should do = generalize this sonic feature to album] *[Note: I'm not sure if this will deserve to be its own paragraph, or whether these ideas will be folded into the previous paragraph. For now, I'm acting as if it will be its own paragraph; I can always revise this later.]* |
| New paragraph 3 showing revised claim tag (bold) and revised function tag (underlined): | **[Revised claim = new paragraph tying time to space: this one particular act of sonic layering also ties temporal dimensions to spatial ones; the supposed "periphery" emerges within the "center."]** [should do = tie temporal dimension of sonic feature to spatial dimension, then explain significance of spatial dimension] |

## Step 7: Assessing Your Aspirational Outline

Assess your aspirational outline using the questions in step 5. Jot notes to yourself as you're working.

Then revise and add to this outline to address what you discovered.

By the end of this step, you should have a final aspirational outline—the one you plan to follow as you revise and continue to draft this section.

## Step 8: Drafting Topic Sentences to Match Your Aspirational Outline

Now you'll begin to flesh out your aspirational outline. For each paragraph, write a topic sentence that accurately expresses its main claim (if what you wrote in step 6 is not yet a topic sentence). You should try to ensure that each topic sentence is in *your* voice (i.e., *not* "Scholar A defines [term] as 'definition.'"). In other words, what *you* have to say should be readily apparent.

## Step 9: Fleshing Out Paragraphs by Drafting or Assembling

At this point, go back to your full draft and import text that fits in your paragraphs. This will likely involve a mixture of copying old paragraphs wholesale (perhaps minus topic sentences) into your new aspirational draft and breaking up old paragraphs between multiple new paragraphs.

Remember that your goal here is just to match the words you have to the new section framework. It's like the act of producing a chapter collage from chapter 14, but instead of fitting paragraphs into relevant sections, you're fitting material (sentences or parts of paragraphs) into relevant paragraphs. Do *not* revise anything you are porting over.

Finally, if there are paragraphs that exist *only* as a tag (or multiple tags), feel free to spend 10–15 minutes fleshing them out with quick writing. Your goal here is not to write perfect prose; it's to get some ideas down on the page.

## Step 10: Revising Your Transitions

Imagine someone *only* read the first and last sentence of each paragraph. (Unfortunately, some of your readers will do this!) Ask yourself:

- Is there a tangible link (especially a repeated term) between each paragraph and the one that follows it?
- Is it clear what new idea each paragraph is adding to the one that precedes it?
- Does *one* (*and only one—doing both would be annoying to the reader!*) of the following cases apply to each set of adjacent paragraphs? (Note: Case #2 applies to my paragraphs above; the phrase "This one particular act of sonic sampling" points directly back to the focus of the previous paragraph.)

> **Case #1**: The conclusion sentence of the preceding paragraph gestures toward the point the next paragraph will make; *or*
> **Case #2**: The topic sentence gestures back to the paragraph that precedes it.

Revise your topic and conclusion sentences to address what you find.

## Step 11: Repeating Steps 1–10 for the Other Body Sections

You should now have a complete section whose paragraphs proceed in a logical order and that make critical claims in your overarching argument. Even though you've revised only at the paragraph level (and the middles of your paragraphs are likely quite rough), you're well on your way to a completed chapter. And by revising with function and claims in mind above all, you are proceeding in one of the most efficient ways possible.

At this point, repeat this chapter's exercises until all of the other body sections are complete. When you finish, you will have a roughly complete version of your book chapter, minus the introduction and conclusion.

## Optional Step 12: Macro Revising, Using Targeted Questions

If you want an additional set of questions to consider, prefer to revise in a less prescribed way, or have already completed steps 1–11 several times and are looking for a more holistic and less linear way of revising any piece at a macro scale, use the questions below.

### Logic and Argumentation

- Are your claims foregrounded? That is, do you have clear claims for each section and paragraph?
- Does each section-level claim support the chapter-level argument?
- Within each section, does each paragraph support the section-level argument?
- If you removed the section headings, would your chapter still make sense? (That is, do you transition smoothly from section to section?)
- Does each paragraph follow logically from the preceding one?
- Where are the weak spots in your logic? Logical leaps?
- Do you sufficiently prove your claims? If not, do you already have the evidence to be able to support them in the near future? If you don't currently have the evidence to support them, how can you modify your claims to match the evidence you have?
- Look specifically at paragraphs or sections where you give your reader direct access to examples to substantiate your claims. Do you over-prove your claims? Could you still back up the same claims with just one example instead of several? What could you cut without jeopardizing your ability to prove your claims?

### Hierarchy

- Are your sections all at a similar level of importance (even if one is shorter than the others)?
- Have any minor threads managed to promote themselves to greater importance? How might you subordinate them?
- Do all of your paragraphs really deserve the space of a paragraph? Could they instead be sentences?

### Organization and Pacing

- Do all of the sections deserve to be sections? Why?
- Does all the material in each section really belong in that section?
- Where might the reader get bored or feel like the pacing is slow?
- Where might the reader struggle to keep up because you present a lot of abstract ideas?

### Shape and Flow

- Do consecutive paragraphs make it easy for the reader to understand in which direction she is moving—abstract to concrete or concrete to abstract?
- What evidence does each section mobilize to support its main claims? Does this evidence truly allow you to make these claims?

## Step 13: Adjusting Your Book Questions and Chapter Answers

Now that you've revised a chapter, look back at your chapter answers. What tweaks do you need to make? How will this impact your book questions and other chapters' answers? Make any necessary revisions to this chapter's answers (and book questions or other chapters' answers, if applicable).

# DEBRIEF, SUPPORT, AND TROUBLESHOOTING

Congratulations! You should now have a rough chapter draft. That is, you have the core of your chapter down on paper and are fairly confident that it's logically sequenced and that each paragraph tangibly advances the argument.

You might be surprised by how quickly you were able to get the core of your chapter into shape, and you may feel more confident that your chapter serves your book's claims.

In chapter 16, you'll subject this chapter to a final set of exercises, designed to help you quickly foreground your voice and sound more confident. After doing so, you can also subject your prose to the targeted questions in appendix F, which will help you revise your paragraphs' sentences.

- ☐ **This is very different from the way I'm used to working, and it's making me uncomfortable. Is this really going to become a chapter?**
  As we said in chapter 14, it can be hard to let go of the idea that revising a chapter means starting at the beginning and making it sound better, one sentence or paragraph at a time. We believe that revising bigger chunks of material first—moving paragraphs around before you focus on sentences or word choice—is the most

efficient way to arrive at claims-driven chapters. Try following this method all the way through to produce a complete chapter draft before you give up on it. Even if not all the steps are useful, keep the basic principles in mind: prioritize your claims, keep track of what you have on the page with some kind of outline, and revise your structure before you copyedit.

☐ **Why can't I just use my normal revising process?**

The revising process you developed before you started this workbook might be well suited to you, and you can always use it instead of the exercises we propose in chapters 14 and 15. We wrote these chapters because many authors we've worked with never developed a systematic revising process, beyond "open my draft and revise sentence by sentence." So we offer these revising exercises as a structured, repeatable way to revise efficiently. If, after trying them, you still prefer your normal way of working, feel free to use it!

| | |
|---|---|
| How did this chapter's exercises give you new insights into your project? | |
| What questions or concerns not found in the list above do you now have about your book? | |

| What might you need to think more about as you go along? Which, if any, choices would you like to revisit later? | |

## CHAPTER 16

# Citing with Confidence

## WHAT TO EXPECT

By this point in the workbook, you've done the work to rethink your book structurally, hierarchize its claims, and ensure that your chapters prioritize these claims.

You can be confident that your book makes a solid, coherent argument. But how can you communicate that confidence to your readers? And if you're leaning so hard on your own argument, how and where should you engage with the work of other scholars, as you know you must?

In the final chapter of this workbook, we're going to answer these questions. We have a theory that many authors can make their book manuscripts sound more "book-like"—more confident, more sophisticated, more elegant—by making some relatively simple changes to the ways they cite other scholars. In this chapter, we'll give you our favorite straightforward tips for citing with confidence while foregrounding your own voice. This isn't a chapter about how to format your references; instead, it's about how to weave other scholars' work into your book without being told you're "citing defensively" or being "excessively deferential to other scholars" or "belaboring your self-positioning in the analysis." You'll likely find this chapter especially useful if you've ever been advised to eliminate "dissertation-ese" from your manuscript.

### Common Discoveries in Chapter 16

- **The fixes are quicker and easier than you'd feared.** Because "engaging with the literature" involves a lot of intellectual work, authors typically fear that making improvements in this area will be complicated. While it's certainly not simple to articulate how your work builds on other scholars' work, many of the common problems authors run into have surprisingly efficient solutions.
- **You begin to feel more like an equal participant in a community of scholars.** This feeling tends to come more slowly for authors of first books, especially if you defended your dissertation recently. You might still struggle to trust that you have something worthwhile to say, but you'll likely at least get glimpses of this confidence as you do the exercises.
- **Your writing sounds more confident.** The strategies you will learn in this chapter can be applied to any type of scholarly writing. While the conventions for a journal article differ from those of a book chapter, you can use these principles to make your other writing sound more confident as well.

## Common Stumbling Blocks

- **Second-guessing citational practices: when, how much, where?** Many scholars feel apprehensive when limiting their citations and start to ask more fundamental questions about what they can claim to "know." Additionally, they feel self-conscious because they think these are questions that should have been addressed much earlier in their scholarly career. In this chapter, we'll outline different ways of thinking about how, when, and why to cite that should reassure you.
- **You feel insecure in claiming your own voice.** This is normal. When you wrote your dissertation, you likely didn't yet feel like an "authority" in your field or on your topic. Moreover, because you were speaking with a smaller group of scholars—likely those who had more claim to "authority" than you—you might underestimate your own claim to authority. It takes time.
- **You worry that reviewers will reject your book because you don't have enough citations (or because you forgot "that one citation").** Remember that your readers come to your book to hear what you have to say. They trust that you're part of a community of scholars. Few readers have enough time to read pieces just to catalogue all of the sources the author *didn't* cite.

## EXERCISES
### Step 1: Deciding Whether and Where to Cite

Let's return to the idea that you are an intellectual tour guide and your book is your tour. Your typical readers come to your intellectual tour with the assumption that you have the requisite knowledge to say something about the material. Since you have your PhD, they presume that you're part of a community of scholars; they are "friendly peers" and people who are genuinely interested in what you have to say. They are *not* merely attending your tour as "gotcha" participants waiting to attack you for the one source you forgot to cite. Nobody has time for that.

Similarly, you can have faith that readers will follow your ideas if they're well expressed. They're attending the tour just to *take* the tour; they are not there to be backseat drivers or to second-guess your tour's construction.

This vision of your audience is crucial to this chapter because we want to encourage you to let go of any anxiety you may have about being criticized for failing to cite comprehensively. This anxiety may be especially pronounced if your book began as a dissertation, because dissertation writers often demonstrate that they know their field by citing other scholars' work widely and at length. When you're writing a book, though, you need to mobilize others' ideas for a different purpose. In your book, you'll cite others' ideas *to advance your claims.*

What does this mean in practice?

Citing secondary sources is an important tool in your argumentative toolkit. But just like any other tool, citation can be used problematically or skillfully. Before reviewing your book manuscript, let's consider several reasons authors cite secondary sources (including direct quoting, paraphrasing, and tangential references) in a book, ranging from more problematic to stronger.

## PROBLEMATIC MOTIVATIONS FOR CITING SCHOLARSHIP
### The Knee-Jerk Exhaustive Impulse

You might have a mental alarm that sounds each time you reference an important person, term, text, event, or concept. It might sound like this: "Oh, I just referenced 'the nation,' so I *must* cite [list of sixteen scholars who have proposed, engaged with, or problematized this concept]." When you think of your book as an intellectual tour, though, it quickly becomes clear why citing this way is counterproductive: readers cannot tell what you (the tour guide) want them to take from this stop, or how this stop fits into the tour's main arc.

### The "Signaling Rigor through Citing Theory" Impulse

Authors of first books often assume that their books must make grand claims or propose new theories to be publishable. This assumption finds its way into these authors' citation practices: many believe that without references to—if not sustained engagement with—canonical theoretical texts in their field, their monograph will be dismissed as not serious enough. This is not the case. Theory, just like any other source, is a *tool* you can use in certain instances to support *your claims*. It is not a marker of or shorthand for scholarly rigor. Your ideas need to be rigorous in their own right.

### The Reactionary Impulse

We'll discuss this impulse in more depth in step 3, but citing one or numerous secondary sources in order to show how your study carves out a (very narrow) piece of scholarly terrain or offers a corrective to previous studies often has an effect that's the opposite of the one you intend, because doing so hinges the significance of the author's ideas on what others have said. In other words, citing this way tends to suggest that your ideas are not significant or worthy of attention on their own.

To put it in the framework of an intellectual tour, this would be the equivalent of a tour guide taking you to the east side of a monument and saying, "Tours A, B, C, and D take people to this monument, but they always stop at the north side. They tell their attendees [information]. But nobody approaches it from the east side, so that's what we're doing." Think about it: either approaching the monument from the east side is significant in its own right—that is, doing so gives us understanding we could not possibly have gleaned by approaching it from the north—or it's not. Similarly, citing scholarship just to point out a gap in the existing literature does not automatically make exploring that gap significant. In books, it's important to show the value of exploring that gap on its own terms.

## STRONGER MOTIVATIONS FOR CITING SCHOLARSHIP

After reading the section above, you might begin to think that you should almost never cite scholarship in your book. That's not the case, though. As we outlined above, citing others' words, ideas, or conclusions is an important tool we can use in making our own arguments; it's just a matter of using this tool for the right reasons. Here are two situations in which citing scholarship is precisely the right tool for the job.

### To Show How You Came to Your Conclusions

Successfully making your book's and chapters' scholarly arguments involves careful attention to logical development, avoiding big leaps. Other scholars' ideas often form key points in your logical development.

Say you're making a claim about how the electrical grid had varied material impacts on residents of Newfoundland in the twenty-first century. Part of making your claim involves asking about power supply, which, in turn, requires probing the question of measurement. So, in constructing your argument, you might first establish that there is enough supply (as shown by Lee), and then synthesize the various conclusions others have drawn about measurement (you agree with Gutierrez, who, in contrast to others, concludes that measuring energy availability must also involve calculating infrastructural leakage), before you can show how this theoretically sufficient supply reaches homes in unequal ways.

One way of thinking about this way of using citations is that it lets you take intellectual shortcuts. When someone else has already written about a history, term, concept, or phenomenon that enriches your analysis, you can cite the scholar efficiently and move on—and be thankful you don't need to research *everything* from scratch.

For instance, say you're writing an analysis of a particular painting to show how it testifies to changing notions of the body in a given historical and geographical context. Part of your argument hinges on showing how this painting reconfigures the relationship between human bodies and the natural environment. You certainly *could* undertake a years-long inquiry to assemble archival historical documents from the time to answer the question "How did people of this time and place think of the relationship between their body and the natural environment?" But if scholars have already done this work, you can save yourself some effort.

## To Point the Reader toward Other Ideas

Some citations, especially in dissertations, tell readers where to learn more about ideas that are related to the book's main intellectual work. Unlike the first kind of citations, these should generally be kept in the notes. For instance, if your study focuses on the effect of technology on northern Italian regional dialects, the question of language preservation might be relevant but tangential. If you were to broach this topic at all, you might include the following note: "For more on twenty-first-century efforts to preserve northern Italian regional dialects, see Pozzi (2011)."

Note that these citations tend to be perceived as less strong because they're not tangibly advancing your chapter's main ideas. If you have to reduce your word count at some point, they should be the first things you cut.

*Want Additional Practice?*

Review at least one section of a model book's chapter. Classify each citation of a secondary source (direct quote, paraphrase, etc.) using the motivations listed above. How many "problematic" impulses do you find? Note particularly striking examples of "stronger" citations and identify what makes them strong.

Remember that readers come to your book interested in what you have to say and assuming that you've mastered the literature enough to be able to make claims. You don't need to cite secondary sources just because they're about relevant topics. Instead, you should cite them in order to make *your* analysis clearer, more efficient, or more compelling.

It's also important to think about *where* you cite other scholars. In a book, we recommend that you cite sources whenever possible at their point of use. Instead of covering all of the relevant secondary literature in your chapter's introduction (or worse, in a "lit review" section), try to weave citations into the chapter at whatever point they're topically relevant. By the same token, don't promote a source to the book introduction if its primary purpose is to support your analysis in a single chapter. Cite sources at the point when they become useful to your analysis, and not before.

Think of it this way: if you, the intellectual tour guide, make your tour attendees listen to a background lecture before the tour begins, they might doze off. A good tour guide will take the guests to a point of interest, call attention to an intriguing feature, and proceed to explain the feature with occasional references to other people's scholarship. Practically, this means that whereas your dissertation may have had multi-paragraph or even multi-page sections devoted to surveying the secondary literature, your book's citations will likely be more evenly distributed.

To assess your citations, choose one chapter to work on: a body chapter, not the book introduction or conclusion or a background chapter. Search the chapter for each citation of a secondary source (including block quotations, direct citations, paraphrases, and passing references). For each one, ask yourself this main question:

*What is my motivation for citing **this source** at **this point** in my book's intellectual tour?*

- Do any of the three "problematic" impulses apply? If so, consider eliminating the citation or citing this source with a different motivation in mind.
- Does this citation give my reader an *essential* piece of the way I arrived at my thinking? Would the reader be able to follow the logic of my argument without it? If you answer "no" to the former or "yes" to the latter, consider eliminating the citation. If you know the citation is important, revise the paragraph in question to clarify how your work builds on the other scholar's.
- Does this citation help me take an intellectual shortcut that strengthens my analysis, or is it just providing tangential information? If it's the latter, consider eliminating it, or at most keeping it in a note.
- Is this the best place for this citation? If it's in the chapter introduction or a background section, is it necessary to set up my chapter-level claims? If not, could I weave it into the chapter's analysis?

## Step 2: Deciding How Much to Cite

To ensure that your ideas remain at the fore, you also need to judiciously deploy secondary sources, rather than simply quoting them extensively. One author put it this way: she tended to block quote (and take the author's point as self-evident) in place of writing out the thinking (in her voice) that she hadn't done yet.

We can't emphasize it enough: when you write your book, things need to be in *your* voice and serve *your* claims. Few people go on a tour hoping to listen to the tour guide read a guidebook aloud. Instead, most of us want to hear the tour guide's synthesized take on the material, perhaps punctuated by particularly useful, illustrative, or well-expressed ideas from others.

In practical terms, you can prioritize your voice by controlling *how much* of your sources you cite.

- In general, avoid block quotes from secondary sources. If you do use a block quote, assume that your reader will skip over it; provide a brief gloss afterward that points out whatever you want your reader to notice. (Then go back and ask yourself whether the block quotation is still necessary.)
- Minimize direct quotes from secondary sources. Aim to quote only when a citation is particularly significant, vivid, or interesting.
- Whenever possible, paraphrase instead of quoting directly. Paraphrasing privileges your voice and indicates a confident mastery of the source material. Of course, when you paraphrase, cite your source properly.
- If you do quote directly, consider quoting something less than a full sentence: a word, a phrase, half a sentence (e.g., "This is an example of what Aissatou Diop calls 'over/writing desire'"). By placing someone else's ideas into the framework of your sentence, you maintain control of the discussion.
- If you find yourself devoting a whole paragraph, or even multiple paragraphs, to a particular scholar's work, ask yourself whether it's really necessary to do so. Sometimes it is! But sometimes such extended engagement is a remnant of the dissertation writer's impulse to carve out intellectual space. In the book, the space is already yours; you don't need to prove yourself. You may be able to reduce the discussion to just a sentence or two. Be sure that *your ideas* drive this extended engagement with a particular scholar and that it's clear to your reader *why* they must know this information about this scholar's work to follow *your logic*. Above all, avoid extended summary.
- If you frequently mention other scholars in the first sentences of your paragraphs, you may be giving them too much of your book's prime real estate. Aim to open your paragraphs with your own ideas and to incorporate the secondary sources somewhere in the middle.
- In general, avoid quoting other scholars in the concluding paragraph of a chapter, and keep citations in general minimal throughout the conclusion.

With these tips in front of you (keeping in mind that they're general advice, and plenty of exceptions are possible), make a second pass through your chapter to assess your use of secondary sources. To facilitate your assessment, you might want to do a search for quotation marks (to bring up any direct quotes) or for parentheses (if you use in-text citations). You could also scan or underline the first sentence of every paragraph.

## Step 3: Deciding How to Cite

Some writers, especially in the humanities, make liberal use of first-person language to position their work in relation to the published literature. Consider the following example:

Building on Soojin Kwon's work on Black European travel literature, I examine the portrayal of Afro-Italian tourism in texts by Nassera Chohra and Jadelin Gangbo. Whereas Kwon focuses primarily on Black British protagonists who travel throughout continental Europe, primarily France, and perform what she calls "Black European touristic comparisons," my work expands the analysis of Black European travel literature to include narrators from Italy and departs from Kwon's definition of travel literature to include semi-autobiographical novels with significant travel components. In so doing, I shift the focus away from Kwon's comparisons between Britain and France and emphasize the Italian characters' assertion of the right to interpret Europe through their touristic gaze.

Notice how many words this author spends justifying his choice of topic and texts in relation to Kwon's. In a dissertation, this careful differentiation might convey confidence. In a book, such extensive use of "positioning" language will likely have the opposite effect: it can be read as overly deferential or defensive posturing, which counterintuitively signals a *lack* of confidence. Notice that it positions others' voices as the animating force behind the author's ideas rather than teaching the reader the author's conclusions about the topic on their own terms.

Remember that readers will presume that you've mastered the scholarship and that you're part of a community of peers. As a member of this community, your job is to use other people's ideas as intellectual tools, not to compare yourself to others to earn a spot (you already belong!) or to push anyone else out. (If you find yourself being harshly critical of another scholar, ask yourself whether their work deserves as much space or energy as you're giving it.)

To revise the passage above, we would condense the references to the secondary source and minimize the use of first-person language. We'd advise this author to breezily cite what's most useful to him, confidently describe his own work, and then move on.

> In her work on Black European travel literature, Soojin Kwon draws attention to what she calls "Black European touristic comparisons." I show how Black Italian narrators of semi-autobiographical novels make such comparisons with the aim of emphasizing their right not just to belong, but also to interpret Europe through their touristic gaze.

If the passage in question occurs somewhere other than the chapter's introduction, we would even encourage this author to eliminate "I show how." Such phrases—*I argue, I show, I demonstrate, this project shows*—are useful for pointing the reader to the argument statement in the chapter introduction. If you use them outside the introduction, they may start to sound like excessive self-positioning. *Stop describing the way you're leading this tour,* your reader may think, *and just tell us about the monuments!* Here's how we would rewrite the passage above as part of a body section:

> In her work on Black European travel literature, Soojin Kwon draws attention to what she calls "Black European touristic comparisons." The Black Italian narrators of *Volevo diventare bianca* and *Verso la notte bakonga* occasionally make such comparisons, emphasizing their right not just to belong, but also to interpret Europe through their touristic gaze.

Look through your chapter and assess the language with which you cite secondary sources, especially your use of first-person language. It may be helpful to do a search for "I" and "my." Ask yourself:

- If I use self-positioning language, is it necessary? Is there a different way I could connect this scholarship to my work?
- Do I sound as though I'm trying (unnecessarily or excessively) to justify my work?

- If I criticize other scholars' work, do I do so efficiently, fairly, and for the purpose of advancing my analysis?
- Am I using this idea as an intellectual tool? Am I conveying confidence that I belong to this community of scholars?

## DEBRIEF, SUPPORT, AND TROUBLESHOOTING

Congratulations! You should now have a structurally solid body chapter that moves your book's claims forward and engages with other scholars' work in a confident voice. In other words, the body sections of the chapter draft now likely "sound like a book"—hopefully in less time than you'd assumed it would take.

☐ **I still worry that reviewers will reject the book because I missed citations.**
Your peer reviewers will likely recommend some scholarship you should engage as you're undertaking your manuscript revisions. But in our experience, if you're doing your due diligence, choosing to not cite something—or even (*gasp*) not knowing about a particular citation—will not be a reason your manuscript gets rejected. In fact, it's common for authors to receive the opposite comment: that they need to "cut any passages that read as lit reviews" or "foreground their voice."

☐ **My chapter still feels quite rough (and is incomplete!).**
You're right that while you've completed a few revising passes (in chapters 14 and 15), you will likely still need to revise and polish your prose before you're ready to call this chapter's body sections "done." We presume that you have some preferred revision strategies that will take your chapter the rest of the way; if you don't (or if you want to try out alternatives), appendix F gives you some ideas. Do, though, keep this workbook's practices in mind as you continue to revise: challenge yourself to work more quickly than you might normally; strive to get to 80 percent; and remember that your work is iterative. We highly recommend sharing your work now (or soon) with a trusted interlocutor, who can help you make sure your chapter is moving in the right direction.

| How did this chapter's exercises give you new insights into your project? | |
|---|---|

| | |
|---|---|
| What questions or concerns not found in the list above do you now have about your book? | |
| What might you need to think more about as you go along? Which, if any, choices would you like to revisit later? | |

# Final Words

This workbook's main purpose has been to help you distill your book's highest-order claims, then use those claims to structure your body sections of your core body chapters. By now, you have accomplished this objective: by completing the exercises in chapters 1–13, you reconceptualized your book and articulated what each chapter does to advance the book's claims. Then, in chapters 14–16, you produced drafts of chapters aligned with your chapter- and book-level priorities and revised them to convey confidence. This is as far as this workbook will take you in revising your book's body chapters (though the exercises in appendix F contain additional revising suggestions).

Beyond the workbook's content, you've also developed four key practices that will serve you well in finishing the book manuscript and beyond. You **prioritized action**—breaking this massive project down, starting before you might have felt ready, and working diligently, despite doubts. You **aimed for progress, not perfection**—a practice that works just as well in other academic writing projects. You **reflected intentionally and captured your doubts** along the way, which helped you see your thinking sharpen over time. And finally, you **built confidence in your project by asking (rather than turning away from) challenging questions**.

Finishing your full book manuscript and navigating the publishing process will bring their own challenges. At this point, though, you have not only a much stronger and intentional project, but also skills you can use long after you finish your first manuscript. We can't wait to hear your stories of success—both large and small!

# ACKNOWLEDGMENTS

The earliest roots of this workbook stretch back to our formative graduate years at UCLA, whose commitment to intellectual excellence and mentorship around teaching and writing—notably in its graduate faculty and the Graduate Writing Center (GWC)—is beyond compare. Our participation in the programming offered by the GWC under the expert guidance of its visionary director Marilyn Gray not only taught us to take an analytical view of the various genres of academic writing, but also shaped our understanding of academic writing as a craft to practice and refine in community over time. We owe special thanks to Dominic Thomas, who chaired both of our dissertations. His generous feedback and guidance—especially about scope and structure—taught us to think about our projects' bigger stakes, with an eye to the published scholarly works they would become. We also owe a tremendous debt of gratitude to Lia Brozgal, who sat on both of our committees and provided the most thorough, insightful, and constructive feedback, without which we would not have grown nearly as much as writers and thinkers. Through countless conversations, Lia not only modeled what it means to be a scholar, thinker, and writer, but also served as a regular sounding board.

This workbook exists because of the openness and generosity of the more than one hundred authors who have worked through these exercises over the years: the online "boot camp" participants and the readers who beta-tested the workbook as we developed it. As we read their feedback and saw how their thinking evolved, we revised the exercises to make them more broadly useful—and so each of these authors, whether named here or not, deserves credit for helping bring this workbook to fruition. Our conversations with the following authors (in no particular order) were particularly formative in the development of the book: Tessa Farmer, Pallavi Sriram, Monika Bhagat-Kennedy, Courtney Sato, Sarah Fong, Desh Girod, Jennifer Park, Taneisha Means, Hannah Waits, Hilary Cooperman, Maggie Elmore, Naomi Macalalad Bragin, Michaelanne Thomas, Martha Balaguera Cuervo, Jocelyn Franklin, Stephanie Bosch Santana, Christina Lord, Cara Snyder, Sudev Sheth, Laura Brade, Gabriella F. Buttarazzi, Crystal Marie Moten, Denva Gallant, Jenny Banh, Elizabeth Saylor, Stephany Cuevas, Alexandra Verini, Manuel Cuellar, Jennifer Darrell, Alysia Garrison, Janine de Novais, Felipe Pruneda Senties, Carla Neuss, and Lee Pierce. Special thanks to Johanna Montlouis-Gabriel and Christopher Bonner for their robust feedback at regular intervals. We're also grateful to the many friends and colleagues who offered support and feedback as these exercises took shape, especially Brittany Asaro, Lucy Swanson, George MacLeod, Michelle Lee, Michelle Bumatay, Hannah Grayson, Annie de Saussure, Zach Smith, and Jennifer Parrack.

Wendy Belcher taught us how to write articles and showed us how valuable a workbook can be, and she, Steven Gump, and Robert Brown gave us crucial encouragement and support at a key point in the book's development. Without their encouragement and keen insight, none of this would have been possible. The stellar team at the University of Chicago Press has worked indefatigably with us to bring this book into the world. Above all, we thank our editors Mary Laur and Mollie McFee, who made this a smoother and more enjoyable process than we had dreamed it could be. The book has also benefited tremendously from the efforts of the meticulous copyeditor Marianne Tatom, production editor Lindsy Rice, promotions manager Carrie Olivia Adams, and marketing manager Jennifer Ringblom. We'd especially like to thank our three anonymous reviewers, whose insightful suggestions showed us how to strengthen the book.

Katelyn:

Because the kernel that became this workbook originates in my own multi-year journey of writing my dissertation and revising it into a book, I would first like to doubly thank those I recognized in my first book's acknowledgments, especially the friends and colleagues without whose support, advice, and enthusiasm I would surely not have finished that book, much less this one. I owe special thanks to Michelle Lee for never-ending support and insightful feedback for almost a decade! Words truly cannot express how fulfilling it was to share in our unflagging support for each other as writers, thinkers, and friends. Everyone should be so lucky.

I owe deep thanks to my UCA Languages, Linguistics, Literatures, and Cultures and College of Arts, Humanities, and Social Sciences faculty and chair colleagues (many of whom have become friends) who have supported and mentored me along the way. To the Office of Research and Sponsored Programs, thanks for sponsoring my book publishing webinar. And to Dean Thomas Williams and Provost Patricia Poulter: thank you for permission to develop and run the summer workshops that became this workbook and for your genuine excitement and enthusiasm about this project as it developed.

Allison—I cannot thank you enough for your support over the years, from our Tea-forest writing sessions to your sharp insight in developing and sharpening this workbook. I still remember the phone call during which I pitched what must have sounded like a wild, half-baked idea—the seed of what eventually became this workbook. It sounds like a platitude, but this book truly would look nothing like it does without your involvement—I and the readers are lucky you took a chance on this project!

To my family: thank you and I love you, now and forever. Thank you, Ken Sterling, Linda Sterling, and Amy and Doug Kirschbaum, for making me feel like part of the family even if my movie-line quoting capacity is still subpar. Aunt Karen, Uncle Dale, Liliha, and Grandma: thank you for your unflagging support and genuine curiosity about my projects. To Christopher Knox: I relish our run-chats, even if you do make me run up ridiculous hills. I am continually in awe of your athletic feats and admire your boundless courage. To my parents, JoAnn and Jeffrey Knox: I don't know how we got so lucky as to have you as parents. You would drop—and have dropped!—everything to support your children, and for that I remain eternally grateful. Kevin: you never cease to amaze me with your ideas, creativity, and compassion. I look forward to seeing the bright and funny young man you become. Finally, to Victor: thanks for being the best husband and partner I could imagine. Your carefree spirit and sense of humor brighten each day, and yes, I promise I'll still like (and always try to finish) your jokes forever.

Allison:

I owe a tremendous debt of gratitude to my editing clients, who have taught me how books work from the inside out and have done me the honor of trusting me with their writing. I'm also deeply grateful to my former professors and colleagues in the UCLA

Comparative Literature and French departments and to the 2012–2015 Harvard History and Literature crew, especially Betsy More, Franny Sullivan, Jennifer Brady, Rachel Gillett, Mo Moulton, and Danny Loss.

To Katelyn: you're the best coauthor I could imagine; thank you a million times for bringing me into this adventure! Collaborating with you has been my favorite part of this project, and I feel unbelievably lucky that the friendship that started in the French TA training seminar has brought us here. Thank you to my dear friends who have listened to me talk about this book during our pandemic backyard get-togethers: Claudia Stumpf, Nathan Paquet, Allie and Aaron Sharpe, Julie Gregorio, Andrew Stout, Eliza and Aaron Griffith, Leah and Adam Questad, and all the kids. These past few years have been so much brighter because of you. I'm also grateful for my other friends who've given me life along the way, especially Marta Antoniolli, Whitney Arnold, Aynne Kokas, Jake and Kelsey Woodruff, Joyce Cannon, Megan Slinkard, Katie Brenner, Edwina Zant, Lisa Meckley, Catherine Vendola, Megan Ryskamp, Laura Saylor, Emilie Guest, and Mike Rolig. A heartfelt thank-you goes out to my family for their love and support: my sisters Erin Patterson, Laura Crumly, and Rebecca Crumly; my brothers-in-law Paul Van Deventer and Joel Patterson; my parents-in-law Allen and Debbie Van Deventer; and above all my parents Jim and Carol Crumly, to whom I'm more grateful than I can possibly express. To Isaac and Theo: I love you dearly, and thank you for being so patient while I was working on this book. And finally, my husband Jim Van Deventer has given me unfailing support and encouragement. Thank you for everything, and I love you.

# APPENDIXES

## APPENDIX A: IF YOUR BOOK ISN'T BASED ON A DISSERTATION

This workbook is designed for authors who are working with a trove of "raw material" for the book manuscript. For many authors, this raw material is a dissertation. Even if the author ends up changing some features of their book (its main claims, its source base, its structure), the experience of having written a preliminary analysis of their source base means that they likely know what they will be able to say about their objects or cases.

If your current book isn't based on a dissertation, you will still be able to use this workbook as long as you have a substantial body of writing to start from. This could be journal articles, conference papers, individual dissertation chapters, and/or the kind of rough draft we guide you to produce in chapter 14.

The exercises in chapters 1–13 are less helpful for authors who have not yet produced a lot of writing about their objects. This is especially true of the two activities at the core of this workbook: producing your book questions and answering them with chapter answers. If you are coming to this work with only an idea for a book—without having done much actual writing, however preliminary—going through the workbook will be an exercise in speculative fiction at best, and a waste of time at worst.

For instance, at the time of this writing, I (Katelyn) am working on my second monograph. While I've kept some of the core ideas from this workbook (like organizing principles and parallelism) in mind as I've been assembling and analyzing my evidence base, I have not begun the chapter 1 work formally because I don't yet know what claims each chapter will be able to develop.

You can use the guidelines below to identify how the workbook might work best for you.

### Readiness Checklist

Use this checklist to identify whether you are ready to work through chapters 1–13 from beginning to end.

- ☐ I know, broadly speaking, what my book as a whole will show.
- ☐ I have settled on a provisional structure.
- ☐ I know the works, case studies, or source bases that will form the basis of 75 percent of my core body chapters (i.e., not my book introduction or conclusion).
- ☐ I have a broader list of works, case studies, or source bases that I *could* draw from, but that, for various reasons, do not belong in this project.
- ☐ I know, concretely, what I will be able to claim in 75 percent of my core body chapters (that is, I've done enough analysis to know what I will be able to show using the evidence I've selected).
- ☐ I have drafty writing (including conference papers, notes, and/or chapter drafts) that corresponds to at least 50 percent of the manuscript. (See chapter 14 for an example of the kind of rough writing we have in mind.) The main idea here is that we want

you to have words—whether ultimately usable in your book or not—down on paper to ensure that your book is anchored in something concrete (and is not purely an abstract idea).

If you weren't able to check all the statements in the checklist above, refer to the "If less than 50 percent of your book has been drafted" section of this workbook's introduction for tips on how to proceed.

## APPENDIX B: IF YOUR SCOPE NEEDS A CLOSER LOOK

You might sense that the terms you use to describe your book's scope are not quite right. This appendix helps you identify other terms you might use to describe your book's geographical scope, historical scope, and evidence base.

In general, the work consists of identifying the terms you currently use, brainstorming other terms you might use, reflecting on which one works best, and then checking that these terms are consistent with what you're doing in your chapters.

1. What term do I currently use to describe my book's geographical scope, historical scope (or periodization), evidence base (people, events, or examples you study), or methodology?

   EXAMPLE GEOGRAPHIES: the urban South, France, the Francophone Caribbean

   EXAMPLE CHRONOLOGIES: the nineteenth century (implies 1800–1899), the interwar period, Maoist

   EXAMPLE EVIDENCE BASE: novels, representations of dance, Southern regional comprehensive universities

2. What alternative terms could I use (broader, narrower, seen through a different lens)?

   EXAMPLE ALTERNATIVES TO "THE URBAN SOUTH": Texas, Arkansas, and Louisiana; the South; Texarkana; the United States; three Southern US states

   EXAMPLE ALTERNATIVES TO "THE NINETEENTH CENTURY": the long nineteenth century (1789–1914); realism (literary periodization); post-Romanticism (literary periodization defined by reactionary nature); 1832–1889 (the exact years of the study)

   EXAMPLE ALTERNATIVES TO "NOVELS": literary fiction, fiction, realist texts, realist literature, works of realism

3. Which term is most appropriate, and why?

   DECISION FOR GEOGRAPHY: Since my study does not talk about some of the most important Southern metropolises (like Atlanta), I actually think the term I've been using is not appropriate for my book's material. I think I might shift to "three urban centers in Southern US states."

   DECISION FOR CHRONOLOGY: Since my book is a literary study, I think "realist" is the best term to describe my evidence base and time period. I will continue to use "the nineteenth century" in many places because it is an important search term.

   DECISION FOR EVIDENCE BASE: I think "novels" continues to work well.

4. Check this term against your chapters by repurposing the question you used when you checked your chapter answers' terminology: Is [chapter-specific term] *really* an

example of [term]? (If you have not yet reached chapter 10, ask how well the term you've decided is most appropriate *also* applies to each individual chapter.)

> REFLECTION FOR GEOGRAPHY: I think making my term "three urban centers in Southern US states" matches my chapters better. None of my chapters falls outside this area.

> DECISION FOR CHRONOLOGY: Since my book's case studies are all considered realist works, this shift is appropriate. One of the threads I develop, though, is that these authors are all reacting to Romanticism, though they're not always all thought of as post-Romantic. So I will develop the idea of post-Romanticism, but I won't use it as my book's main term.

> DECISION FOR EVIDENCE BASE: Now that I think about it, each chapter studies several texts (essays, critical pieces, letters) that are not technically novels. However, my book's main purpose is to make claims about the fictional texts; I use the other writings as important contextualizing information. So, when I'm presenting my book's claims, I should use the word "novels," but when I describe my broad evidence base, I will need to be careful to use a term flexible enough to include essays, critical pieces, and letters. Perhaps a list? Or "writing—fictional, nonfictional, and epistolary"?

## APPENDIX C: IF YOU'RE UNSURE ABOUT YOUR ORGANIZING PRINCIPLE QUESTION

If you aren't sure that the question your organizing principle implies is truly the question at the heart of your book, an alternative place to start is with your topic.

### Step 1: Reprising Your Topic Statement

Return to the table in chapter 1 where you recorded your book's topic and write down the topic statement verbatim, like this. It's fine if your topic statement is not a complete sentence (or if it's multiple sentences) or if you realize it's "not quite right"—we'll fix it soon enough.

**HISTORY**

| Topic Statement: | The second wave of emigration from the Eastern Bloc, 1986–1987 |
|---|---|

**LITERARY STUDIES**

| Topic Statement: | twentieth-century Scandinavian literary innovation |
|---|---|

**POLITICAL SCIENCE**

| Topic Statement: | BIPOC mayors and racial representation |
|---|---|

**HISTORY/HISTORIOGRAPHY**

| Topic Statement: | The (re)writing of South Sudanese national history and memory post-2011 |
|---|---|

**LITERARY STUDIES**

| Topic Statement: | Feminism and secular patriotism in Rita Cetina Gutiérrez's fiction, journalistic writings, and educational work |
|---|---|

**SOCIOLOGY**

| Topic Statement: | The lived, domestic experiences of the pre-Google internet in suburban US households, 1994–1998 (Google released in 1998) |
|---|---|

Now it's your turn.

| Topic Statement: | |
|---|---|

If your topic statement is a series of statements, you must choose one before moving on.

## Step 2: Review—Who's Doing What to Whom?

By the end of this step, you should have a clearer statement of what the reader should take away (as a content lesson) about this topic.

Regardless of whether the book studies recognizable people or groups, your book's main idea will need to be formulated as a complete, albeit very basic, sentence with a subject, a verb, and likely a direct object.

If your topic statement is not yet a full sentence, use the "who's doing what to whom" model to transform what you have into a full sentence. You might find that it's easiest to draft this statement by starting directly with the subject. If that doesn't feel quite right, you can consider beginning with "how."

Note: If this exercise feels difficult, ask yourself whether your topic statement mobilizes too many "big concepts" (identity, patriarchy, belonging, embodiment, etc.). If you suspect this might be the case, split the statement into several more concrete topic statements. Then return to exercise 1 above.

| Original Topic Statement | Who's Doing What to Whom? (New Statement) |
|---|---|
| The second wave of emigration from the Eastern Bloc, 1986–1987 | **International organizations** facilitated the second wave of emigration from the Eastern Bloc, 1986–1987. |
| twentieth-century Scandinavian literary innovation | **Twentieth-century Scandinavian novelists** developed innovative literary styles. |
| BIPOC mayors and racial representation | **BIPOC mayors** represent minority interests to varying degrees and in different ways. |
| The (re)writing of South Sudanese national history and memory post-2011 | South Sudanese **historians** and **publics** (re)write national history and memory post-2011. |

| Feminism and secular patriotism in Rita Cetina Gutiérrez's fiction, journalistic writings, and educational work | **Rita Cetina Gutiérrez** developed her own brand of feminism and secular patriotism through fiction, journalistic writings, and educational work. |
| --- | --- |

Now, double-check that the actor (subject) and action (verb) capture what you're most interested in studying at the book level.

For instance, the author of the first new statement above would ask herself whether her book is *really* most interested in tracing how *international organizations facilitated* escape, or whether they're *actually* most interested in studying how *emigrants navigated* the constraints and opportunities of international organizations.

### Step 3: Checking against the Question Implied by the Organizing Principle

You should now have a clearer statement that better reflects your book's core priorities. Before proceeding, check your organizing principle to make sure the statement you just drafted is compatible with it.

Take a few minutes to reflect using the prompt below.

| Look back at the question your organizing principle implies. How similar is it to the statement you just drafted? Is the organizing principle still well equipped to support the statement you just drafted? | |
| --- | --- |

If you find that you have strayed significantly from the question your organizing principle implies—to the point that you're no longer sure that your organizing principle will support your statement—return to the start of chapter 2. Work through the activities quickly with this new insight in mind, and consider how (if at all) you might be able to revise the organizing principle to ensure that this claim will work with the book. Be sure to keep in mind the time and resources you will have to undertake such a major book revision.

If, by contrast, your claim works well with your organizing principle, return to and finish chapter 2 (start at step 5).

## APPENDIX D: IF YOUR BOOK QUESTION AND CHAPTER ANSWER TERMS NEED A CLOSER LOOK

When producing and revising your book questions and chapter answers, you might have sensed that some of the terms you use might not be quite right, or you might have wanted targeted exercises to probe your terms further.

If you know which terms you want to test, start by adding them to a table like those you see below. To identify other terms you might scrutinize, review the materials you produced in chapters 1–4 to capture a list of key book-level concepts—those that animate the book as a whole, appearing consistently throughout your chapters.

Then subject your key terms to scrutiny by asking whether they're really the most appropriate for the large concepts or processes you investigate. Many authors of first books resist doing this exercise—or at least they are somewhat anxious about what they might find. Specifically, they worry that once they start to scrutinize their book's key concepts, the house of cards that is their book will start to collapse.

It's true that you might discover that the vocabulary you've been using isn't quite right for the processes you're investigating. Keep in mind, however, that editors, peer reviewers, and book reviewers will be placing your key book concepts under scrutiny later. It's much better to ask these hard questions of your book now, while you're still in a position to consider alternate terms and/or justify the ones you use, than it is to discover only after your book is finished that its terminology is fundamentally flawed.

## HISTORY

| Key term(s)/ concept(s): | Patriarchy/masculine power structure/power |
|---|---|
| Related concepts/terms: | Male dominance, gender inequality, system of male dominance |
| Most appropriate term and why: | I will stick with "patriarchy" at the book level because it captures the broad range of systemic issues I will be exploring in the Senate. Gender inequality does not accurately capture the systemic nature, and male dominance suggests something slightly different. Power is too broad, and masculine power structure is too clunky. The patriarchy is an accessible term for my audience. |
| Complete definition: | The collection of structures, attitudes, beliefs, and effects that maintain a male-dominated power structure |

## ANTHROPOLOGY

| Key term(s)/ concept(s): | Actifoodism (a term I am coining) |
|---|---|
| Related concepts/terms: | Activism, food activism, environmental justice plus economic, social, and embodied empowerment |
| Most appropriate term and why: | I will stick with "actifoodism" at the book level because it allows me to discuss in one word a broad range of activities, including seeking environmental justice and engaging in economic, social, and embodied empowerment. Activism is too broad, and food activism suggests something slightly different from what is going on here. |
| Complete definition: | The range of activities community gardeners engage in to seek environmental justice and engage in their own and their community's economic, social, and embodied empowerment |

## YOUR BOOK

| Key term(s)/ concept(s): | |
|---|---|
| | |

| Related concepts/terms: | |
|---|---|
| Most appropriate term and why: | |
| Complete definition: | |

## APPENDIX E: IF YOU WANT STRATEGIES FOR DRAFTING NEW WORK

More than any other phase of academic writing, the drafting stage is messy, nonlinear, and highly subjective. *Use what works for you!* If you're having trouble starting or want more structured strategies, try these.

### Strategy 1: Close Reading

If you already have solid chapter answers for your chapter, you know which evidence base or case studies you will mobilize, and you are already familiar with your evidence, then your go-to first strategy should be to analyze your evidence in writing.

To begin, choose one passage (or piece of a primary source) that you expect to discuss at some length in your chapter. Set a timer for 25 minutes and make observations about that evidence.

**Sample Actionable Session Goals:**
- Do a close reading of passage A through the lens of B.
- Annotate passage C, circling every instance of direct address, underlining every instance of diction I'd like to engage with, and writing notes about key words, phrases, and rhythm.
- Rewatch sequence D, taking notes about framing/lighting/sound and character movement in each shot.
- Describe image E generally, then unpack the use of color in this image (compared to other contemporaneous works).
- Review participants' interviews through the lens of agency. Categorize their responses into different conceptions of agency (3–5), then explain how the terminology they use leads me to these conclusions.
- Review the use of "nation" in archival sources F, G, and H. Explain how each conceives of the nation and how these conceptions differ.
- Present and discuss the comments about children's museums from interviewees I and J.

## Strategy 2: Asking and Answering Questions

Having a concrete question to answer often helps authors produce writing from scratch. As you're writing, consider keeping a rolling list of questions you think your chapter must answer. To produce pieces of your chapter, write down one of the questions, and then answer it in informal prose. Many authors have found it helpful to write a question or prompt *the day before* their writing session: they find that it helps their ideas marinate.

**Sample Actionable Session Goals:**

- Spend 5 minutes brainstorming a list of topics you believe your section will need to address. Then choose one and spend 25 minutes meditating on the topic in writing.
- At the end of a longer session (90 minutes to 2 hours) during which you've been immersed in your evidence, set a timer. Spend 10 minutes brainstorming a list of questions you have about it. Then take a 5-minute break. When your break is over, set a second 10-minute timer and write down all the questions that now come to mind. You will initially think you have nothing left to ask, but this second session is where you will find the most interesting and fruitful questions. In a subsequent session, choose one question to answer.
- Choose a question from a rolling list of questions and answer it in very rough prose for 15–25 minutes.

## Strategy 3: Distilling Your Evidence Base

If you aren't yet sure which specific pieces of evidence you will discuss at length in your chapter, try writing your way through the evidence base as a whole.

Use the following prompts to generate ideas about your evidence base.

- Make a list of the main themes or questions that emerge from your evidence base, case studies, or primary sources as a whole. Then choose one theme or question and write a preliminary description of how it plays out in your evidence. As you do, make a list of especially rich documents or passages that exemplify this idea.
- Sort your evidence by one characteristic (document type, language, year, author, nationality, etc.). What common features do you notice when you sort in this way?
- Search your source base for one of your chapter's central concepts. In what contexts does it come up? In what contexts is it absent? What patterns do you notice?

## Strategy 4: Dumping Everything You Know

This strategy serves two purposes. First, it helps remind you that you *do* actually know a lot about your topic (often authors of first books don't feel like "experts"). Second, because you're writing things in your own words, it will help you write your eventual chapter in your own "voice."

Here are some ways to approach this strategy. Pick only the ones that seem useful or generative for you. If any of them make you think "I don't know any of that!," skip them. Set a timer for 25 minutes and see how quickly you can get your ideas down on the page.

**Sample Actionable Session Goals:**

- Write everything you know about the geographic/historical context for this section (or for a particular event or work).

- Write everything that comes to mind about the text/case study you'll be studying (this is *not* the time to read; just dump).
- Write everything you know about a central topic you will explore.
- Write everything you know about a central discussion in your field in which your work participates.

### Strategy 5: Explaining to Yourself What You See

This strategy is similar to others (especially "close reading" and "guided freewrites"), but its slightly different framing can help some authors overcome roadblocks.

First, cultivate "beginner's mind" about the works or source bases you plan to use in your chapter. Describe the evidence in objective terms. For the purposes of this activity, *nothing* is too obvious.

Then notice: What intrigues you? Surprises you? What seems important? Why? What do you wonder? Each of the answers can turn into a guided freewrite and, eventually, analyses.

### Strategy 6: Talking as Thinking

Some of my (Katelyn's) most clarifying moments have come when I try to explain my evidence base or case studies to other people, especially those outside my immediate field. This strategy's success depends on the care you take to select an interlocutor; prioritize someone who is genuinely curious, listens well (does not interrupt), and sees their role as helping you understand your ideas on their own terms.

Here are some questions an interlocutor can ask you to help you produce generative writing orally:

- Tell me what you've been finding. Tell me what you think is going on in your evidence base/case studies.
- What have you been working through this week?
- What's jumped out at you in your project?
- What are you unsure about?
- What are you having a hard time articulating?
- What seems not quite right to you?
- What's been on your mind as you're working through this evidence base?

### Strategy 7: Using a Topical Outline

Though Robert Boice has found that incredibly messy "generative writing" works for many authors, some find this approach overwhelming.[1]

If you prefer to work with more structure, try starting with a topical outline and treat each unit as a guided freewrite. If it helps, you can also dump quotes from primary and secondary sources into this topical outline, and then close-read them to flesh out the paragraphs.

## APPENDIX F: IF YOU WANT SOME TOOLS FOR MICRO REVISING

In chapter 15, we helped you complete several macro revising activities, which focused on the paragraphs as the smallest functional units. A micro revising pass focuses on the paragraph level and below and helps you identify lower-order concerns. You can use these questions to guide your revisions *after* you've completed the exercises in chapters 15 and 16.

Here are some questions you can keep in mind as you read through your chapter draft:

## Considering the Topic Sentence

- Does the paragraph's topic sentence make an arguable claim? If not, how could you revise it to foreground your voice and ideas?
- Consider the actor, action, and direct object (if any) of the topic sentence.
  - Check them for accuracy. Do they accurately reflect this paragraph's core idea?
  - Is the actor short and concrete, or is it an abstract noun? Could you revise the actor to be concrete?
  - Does the action immediately follow the actor? If there is an intervening phrase or clause, could you rearrange the sentence so that the actor and action are closer together?
- Does the topic sentence contain *either* a word from the previous paragraph *or* an explicit logical connecting word (just as, unlike, consequently, although, etc.) to signal how the idea in this paragraph relates to what you discussed in the previous paragraph?

## Considering the Paragraph, Globally

- Consider the connections between sentences (what Williams calls "cohesion").[2] Does each sentence contain *either* a word from the previous sentence *or* an explicit logical connecting word (just as, unlike, consequently, although, etc.) to signal how the idea in this sentence relates to what you discussed in the previous sentence?
- Review your logical connecting words. Does each *actually* reflect the relationship between the ideas? For instance, did you use "moreover" (which indicates you are signaling a similarity between ideas *and* amplifying the second point), when you really mean to restate the idea (and so might use "put differently" instead)?
- Think about the structure and shape of this collection of sentences. Is each sentence short and declarative? Or are most of them long, compound-complex sentences? How might you combine (using subordination) or split sentences to create a more dynamic and varied paragraph?

## Considering Each Sentence

- Consider the placement of the actor and action. Are they within seven words of each other (ideally next to each other)?
- Does less important, familiar, or unsurprising information appear toward the beginning of the sentence, and does more important, unfamiliar, or surprising information appear toward the end?
- Think about structure and subordination. Are the sentence's most important ideas presented in the main (independent) clause? Are less important ideas subordinated (presented in parentheticals, dependent clauses, or phrases)?

## Additional Resources for Micro Revising

- Eric Hayot's chapter "The Uneven U" in *The Elements of Academic Style: Writing for the Humanities*.[3] This chapter elaborates a novel framework for thinking about the "shape" of paragraphs, though it is also applicable to writing at other scales (such as a section in a chapter or a chapter in a book). Use these principles to analyze and revise the shape of your paragraphs.

- Joseph M. Williams's chapter "Lesson 5: Cohesion and Coherence," especially pp. 65–68, in *Style: Lessons in Clarity and Grace*, 12th ed.[4] Williams's concept of cohesion—how well sentences flow from one to the next—is a must-know for academic authors.

- Wendy Belcher's "Belcher Diagnostic Test," described in chapter 11 of *Writing Your Journal Article in Twelve Weeks: A Guide to Academic Publishing Success*.[5] Belcher's process helps you tighten your prose. You should use it as a final polishing resource.

- Helen Sword's "Writer's Diet Test" (https://writersdiet.com/test/) is a free diagnostic tool that will help you identify the major areas to improve in your writing. For ways to fix the problems it identifies, consult Sword's *The Writer's Diet: A Guide to Fit Prose*.[6]

# NOTES

## INTRODUCTION

1. At the end of the introduction, we show you how to tailor this workbook's exercises if you already have a book contract or still need to research and draft a lot of your book.

2. William Germano, *From Dissertation to Book*, 2nd ed. (Chicago: University of Chicago Press, 2013), 18–59.

3. William Germano, *On Revision: The Only Writing That Counts* (Chicago: University of Chicago Press, 2022); Germano, *From Dissertation to Book*.

4. Eric Hayot, *The Elements of Academic Style: Writing for the Humanities* (New York: Columbia University Press, 2014); Joseph M. Williams, *Style: Lessons in Clarity and Grace*, 12th ed. (New York: Pearson, 2016); Helen Sword, *Stylish Academic Writing* (Cambridge, MA: Harvard University Press, 2012).

5. Laura Portwood-Stacer, *The Book Proposal Book: A Guide for Scholarly Authors* (Princeton, NJ: Princeton University Press, 2021); William Germano, *Getting It Published: A Guide for Scholars and Anyone Else Serious about Serious Books*, 3rd ed. (Chicago: University of Chicago Press, 2016); Beth Luey, ed., *Revising Your Dissertation: Advice from Leading Editors*, rev. ed. (Berkeley: University of California Press, 2008).

6. Portwood-Stacer, *The Book Proposal Book*.

7. Germano, *Getting It Published*; Luey, *Revising Your Dissertation*; Portwood-Stacer, *The Book Proposal Book*.

## CHAPTER ONE

1. Amy Benson Brown, "The Stages of Revising a Dissertation into a Book," *Journal of Scholarly Publishing* 52, no. 3 (2021): 128; Francess G. Halpenny, "The Thesis and the Book," in *The Thesis and the Book: A Guide for First-Time Academic Authors*, ed. Eleanor Harman et al. (Toronto: University of Toronto Press, 2003), 7; Beth Luey, "Introduction: Is the Publishable Dissertation an Oxymoron?," in Luey, *Revising Your Dissertation*, 5; William P. Sisler, "You're the Author Now," in Luey, *Revising Your Dissertation*, 20; Jennifer Crewe, "Caught in the Middle: The Humanities," in Luey, *Revising Your Dissertation*, 133.

## CHAPTER THREE

1. For a fascinating discussion of pioneer mother monuments in the American West, see Cynthia Culver Prescott, *Pioneer Mother Monuments: Constructing Cultural Memory* (Norman: University of Oklahoma Press, 2019).

## CHAPTER TWELVE

1. Wendy Belcher, *Writing Your Journal Article in 12 Weeks: A Guide to Academic Publishing Success*, 2nd ed. (Chicago: University of Chicago Press, 2019), 67.

## CHAPTER FOURTEEN

1. Robert Boice, *Professors as Writers: A Self-Help Guide to Productive Writing* (Stillwater, OK: New Forums Press, 1990).

## CHAPTER FIFTEEN

1. We're grateful to Marilyn Gray, the director of the UCLA Graduate Writing Center, for teaching us the technique of reverse outlining.

2. Hayot, *The Elements of Academic Style*.

## APPENDIXES

1. Boice, *Professors as Writers*.

2. Williams, *Style*.

3. Hayot, *The Elements of Academic Style*, 59–73.

4. Williams, *Style*, 64–78.

5. Belcher, *Writing Your Journal Article*, 310–326.

6. Helen Sword, *The Writer's Diet: A Guide to Fit Prose* (Chicago: University of Chicago Press, 2016).

# BIBLIOGRAPHY

Belcher, Wendy. *Writing Your Journal Article in Twelve Weeks*. 2nd ed. Chicago: University of Chicago Press, 2019.

Benson Brown, Amy. "The Stages of Revising a Dissertation into a Book." *Journal of Scholarly Publishing* 52, no. 3 (2021): 127–140.

Boice, Robert. *Professors as Writers: A Self-Help Guide to Productive Writing*. Stillwater, OK: New Forums Press, 1990.

Crewe, Jennifer. "Caught in the Middle: The Humanities." In *Revising Your Dissertation: Advice from Leading Editors*, rev. ed., edited by Beth Luey, 131–147. Berkeley: University of California Press, 2008.

Germano, William. *From Dissertation to Book*. 2nd ed. Chicago: University of Chicago Press, 2013.

———. *Getting It Published: A Guide for Scholars and Anyone Else Serious about Serious Books*. 3rd ed. Chicago: University of Chicago Press, 2016.

———. *On Revision: The Only Writing That Counts*. Chicago: University of Chicago Press, 2022.

Halpenny, Frances G. "The Thesis and the Book." In *The Thesis and the Book: A Guide for First-Time Academic Authors*, edited by Eleanor Harman, Ian Montagnes, Siobhan McMenemy, and Chris Bucci, 1–10. Toronto: University of Toronto Press, 2003.

Harman, Eleanor, Ian Montagnes, Siobhan McMenemy, and Chris Bucci, eds. *The Thesis and the Book: A Guide for First-Time Academic Authors*. Toronto: University of Toronto Press, 2003.

Hayot, Eric. *The Elements of Academic Style: Writing for the Humanities*. New York: Columbia University Press, 2014.

Luey, Beth. "Introduction: Is the Publishable Dissertation an Oxymoron?" In *Revising Your Dissertation: Advice from Leading Editors*, rev. ed., edited by Beth Luey, 1–16. Berkeley: University of California Press, 2008.

Luey, Beth, ed., *Revising Your Dissertation: Advice from Leading Editors*. Rev. ed. Berkeley: University of California Press, 2008.

Portwood-Stacer, Laura. *The Book Proposal Book: A Guide for Scholarly Authors*. Princeton, NJ: Princeton University Press, 2021.

Prescott, Cynthia Culver. *Pioneer Mother Monuments: Constructing Cultural Memory*. Norman: University of Oklahoma Press, 2019.

Sisler, William P. "You're the Author Now." In *Revising Your Dissertation: Advice from Leading Editors*, rev. ed., edited by Beth Luey, 17–23. Berkeley: University of California Press, 2008.

Sword, Helen. *Stylish Academic Writing*. Cambridge, MA: Harvard University Press, 2012.

———. *The Writer's Diet: A Guide to Fit Prose*. Chicago: University of Chicago Press, 2016.

Williams, Joseph M. *Style: Lessons in Clarity and Grace*. 12th ed. New York: Pearson, 2016.

# INDEX